Art Nouveau

FROM
MACKINTOSH TO LIBERTY

Charles Rennie Mackintosh,
Glasgow School of Art:
Wrought iron finial on the
eastern tower, 1897-99

right:
Liberty & Co, "the Magnus,"
Cymric silver and enamel
clock, Birmingham, 1930

opposite:
Liberty & Co, Cymric gold
and enamel pendant

Art Nouveau

FROM MACKINTOSH TO LIBERTY

THE BIRTH OF A STYLE

Victor Arwas

ANDREAS PAPADAKIS PUBLISHER

This book is dedicated to my wife Gretha with much love

Cover: Design inspired by a stencilled mural by Charles Rennie Mackintosh designed for the Buchanan St. Tearooms
Back flap: Gerald Moira, Mural above the stage of the Wigmore Hall, London

Designed by Vicky Braouzou
for Andreas Papadakis Publisher

First published in Great Britain in 2000 by
ANDREAS PAPADAKIS PUBLISHER
An imprint of New Architecture Group Limited
107 Park Street
London W1K 7JE

ISBN 1 901092 19 4 (Paperback)
ISBN 1 901092 33 X (Hardback)

Printed and bound in Singapore

CONTENTS

ACKNOWLEDGMENTS   6

INTRODUCTION   9

GLASGOW   19

DUNDEE   70

LONDON   72

LIBERTY STYLE   90

BIRMINGHAM   152

ENAMELS   166

BOOKS: BINDINGS, ILLUSTRATIONS AND BOOKPLATES   174

SCULPTURE   180

BIOGRAPHIES   184

BIBLIOGRAPHY   198

CREDITS   199

INDEX   200

ACKNOWLEDGMENTS

I should like to express my grateful thanks to the many galleries, institutions and collectors who have kindly supplied me with illustrations, particularly Andrew Mackintosh Patrick and Peyton Skipwith of The Fine Art Society; John S.M. Scott; Brad Pitt; Nicholas Harris; John Jesse; Mrs Barbara Macklowe; Andrew Cox; Mrs Fay Lucas; Mrs Gulderen Tekvar; Sonya and David Newell-Smith of Tadema Gallery; Mike Bruce; Keith Baker; Brian Thompson and Derek Rothers of the Millinery Works; Janis and William Wetsman; Geoffrey Diner; The Birkenhead Collection; Anna Buruma and Jo Raw at the Archives of Liberty Plc; Peter Trowles, Taffner Curator, Mackintosh Collection, Glasgow School of Art; Philippe Garner, Lydia Creswell-Jones and Corinna Villinger at Sotheby's, London; Mark Oliver at Phillips, London; Angela Minshull at Christie's Images Ltd; Steve Thomas at the Wigmore Hall; Laura Valentine, Photographic Archive, Royal Academy of Arts; Maria de Beyrie; and all those who wish to remain anonymous. I am equally grateful to Vicky Braouzou for her design; Matt Pia and Michael Todd-White for photography; Ms Fumiko Noro, Director of the Japan Art and Culture Association and her staff for all the kindnesses shown to me and my wife over the long period during which *The Liberty Style* exhibition was being organised by us in conjunction with Professor Anthony Jones, President of the School of the Art Institute of Chicago and Ms Claire Catterall and during its tour of eight museums in Japan.

opposite:
Charles Rennie Mackintosh, The Hill House, drawing room

INTRODUCTION

opposite:
*Frances Macdonald McNair,
Frontispiece for* Das
Eigenkleid *by Anna
Muthesius, Drawing*

The conjunction between Anglo-Scottish crafts design towards the end of the nineteenth century and Art Nouveau is bizarre, adventitious and, in a curious way, inevitable. All the creative designers expressed their detestation of Art Nouveau in no uncertain fashion. That did not stop the French from calling the movement "Modern Style," spelled and pronounced as in English; and French commentators and critics, writing about Art Nouveau buildings, referred to them as being "in the English style." In Italy Art Nouveau was called "Liberty Style," after the name of the London shop. All of which was a clear indication that the Anglo-Scottish designers were creating their own version of Art Nouveau while simultaneously vilifying it.

The first stirrings of a renewed artistic sensibility in Britain occurred not as a rejection of the past, but as an attempt to make it slightly less formal, slightly more human. A combination of emotional openness to artistic currents which were being explored in various countries and improved technical equipment and teaching, both diffused through new magazines, exposed artists in London, Birmingham, Liverpool and Glasgow to the same influences as artists living in Paris, Brussels, Munich, Vienna or Helsinki. Even as artists rejected what they saw illustrated, they were being influenced in subliminal fashion.

A small, but well-chosen collection of Art Nouveau furniture by Gallé and Majorelle and some objects were purchased by a Mr. Donaldson at the 1900 Paris Exhibition and donated to the South Kensington Museum (now the Victoria & Albert Museum). Although the Museum directors tried hard to reject this donation, it was eventually accepted and put on temporary display before being consigned to their depot for many years until rescued in the second half of the twentieth century by creative curators. "After the last Paris Exhibition," wrote T.G. Jackson, R.A. in *The Magazine of Art*, "a collection of furniture in this new style was shown at the South Kensington Museum, and afterwards circulated through the country at the various centres of industry, to inspire them with new ideas. Against this the

Frances Macdonald
MacNair (attributed),
Spring c.1900-05
Watercolour on linen

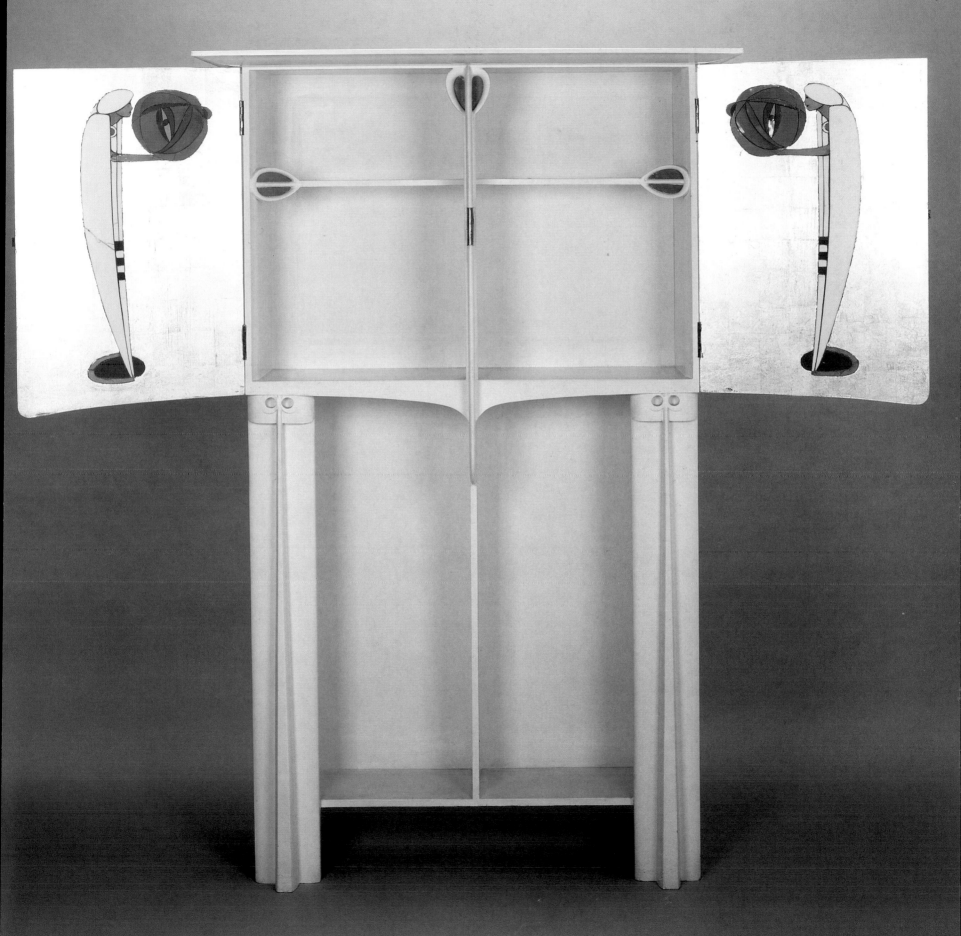

best rendering is full of repose, and quiet unobtrusive beauty."

All the commentators seem to have taken the literal translation of *Art Nouveau* as 'New Art,' although the term, taken from the name of Siegfried Bing's gallery in Paris, actually meant 'contemporary art.' But that expression would equally have induced apoplexy in those same commentators.

Art Nouveau did not reject the past: it reinterpreted it. Nature was its ideal, and the careful study of botany, of fauna, of the insect world, was its foundation. The rigid stylisation of the recent past was replaced by a softer line, fanciful, graceful, organic, inspired by tendril and liana, caress and whiplash. In Britain inspiration came from Celtic art, Continental asymmetry of inter-twining lines replaced by the symmetrical interlacing of the entrelac. The Glasgow Style is often defined as being rectilinear in opposition to the Franco-Belgian curvilinear style, but that is a nonsense. The Glasgow style epitomised by The Four (Mackintosh, the Macdonald sisters, and McNair) and their followers was stylised but practical;

walls, chairs, beds, needed to be rectilinear – where a straight line was not a practical necessity, the curve was often adopted, from design motifs to extravagant shapes. Later products of the Glasgow designers were influenced by German and Austrian straight lines which were the beginnings of Art Deco.

Illustrated art magazines, such as *The Studio* in Britain, *Jugend* in Germany, *Art et Décoration* in France, introduced the work of interesting designers and helped propagate the style. Art Nouveau was not confined to any one thing; furniture, metalwork, glass, ceramics, jewellery, wallpaper, tapestries, carpets were designed to fit the style, and this applied to the slightest products: inkwells, table lamps, clocks, paper-knives, fenders and sconces. As the style became more popular, there was an inevitable flood of derivative objects produced cheaply for the 'popular' market. While most of these have been deservedly consigned to the rubbish bin of history, some of them have acquired the kitsch patina of collectability and a new, perhaps precarious, lease of life.

*above left: Vernon March,
The Faun in Love, bronze on
wood plinth*

*above right: S.M. Wien,
Nude and Lizard, bronze on
ebonised wood plinth*

The creators of Art Nouveau always insisted that they sought to create beauty; but then so have the disciples of most art movements in history, the only differences being in their definition of beauty. Beauty in Art nouveau tends to be ethereal, idealised, mystical and mysterious, imbued with hidden meanings, suffused with longing, yearning and the search for perfection. The French Nabis painters following Gauguin, the Symbolist painters, sculptors, poets and novelists, all contributed to the creation of the Art Nouveau image. The quintessential Art Nouveau nymph in the works of Mucha, Privat-Livemont, Grasset, Berthon or Orazi are directly related to the stunners of Dante Gabriel Rossetti, Frederick Sandys and Evelyn de Morgan, their softly plastic limbs derived from Burne-Jones.

Art Nouveau was never a rigidly monolithic style: it was a clutch of styles, each suited to its originators, but with a certain *air de famille* which, for a few short years, brought about an exciting, creative current of experimentation into architecture, interiors and all aspects of design. Much of it developed in the final decade of the nineteenth century. The early twentieth century was a ferment of creativity: breathtaking Art Nouveau was emerging from Nancy, from Paris, from Brussels, from Glasgow and London, but it was also the time of emergence of the Fauves painters, of Cubism and the *Section d'or*, of the Secessionists in Austria, Germany, Italy, Hungary and Scandinavia as well as the development of what was later to be called Art Deco. All this was to be blown apart by the outbreak of the First World War in 1914, but even before then the deaths of so many of the original Art Nouveau designers had begun the deflation of the style. After the war most of the surviving designers moved on to other styles.

The only thing all the creators of Art Nouveau had in common was a deep antipathy to the movement as it seemed to be proclaimed. And by their very creativity they transformed it into what we now identify as Art Nouveau, with all its expressive extravagance, its exquisite simplicities and its outrageous shafts of beauty.

GLASGOW

Glasgow at the end of the nineteenth century was a wealthy city, with a sophisticated grasp of current international art movements. Several Glasgow artists, including George Henry, James Guthrie, Joseph Crawhall, T. Millie Dow, Stuart Park, Edward Atkinson Hornel, R. Macauley Stevenson, E.A. Walton and John Lavery had formed themselves as a Society in 1887, and they were to exhibit as a group at the Grosvenor Gallery Summer Show in 1890 in London, an exhibition that was to be the start of their international fame. The emphasis of this 'Glasgow School' of painting was on decorative patterns on flat surfaces. In later years they were to be known as 'The Glasgow Boys.'

In 1885 Francis Henry Newberry was appointed Headmaster of the Glasgow School of Art and Haldane Academy. The School had been officially recognised by the government as early as 1844, and in the year Newberry was appointed Headmaster it had reached third place in Great Britain in the number of national medals awarded to its students, with Birmingham in first place and Lambeth, in London, second. The son of a shoemaker, Newberry was an Englishman, born in Membury, Devon, in 1855, though he had spent most of his childhood in Bridport, Dorset. He had studied at its School of Art, later teaching there. Art education in Britain was then centralised in a system set up by Sir Henry Cole in 1852. Students of art were able to teach in ordinary schools while pursuing their studies, after which they could teach in art schools. Newberry taught in various London schools while studying at the National Art Training Schools at South Kensington, eventually teaching drawing and painting and lecturing on anatomy there.

The emphasis at Glasgow was on the fine arts, and Newberry himself was a painter, but he was well aware of the report of the Royal Commission on Technical Instruction, published in 1884, which had concluded that "Industrial design has not received sufficient attention in art schools and classes ... a great departure in this respect from the intention

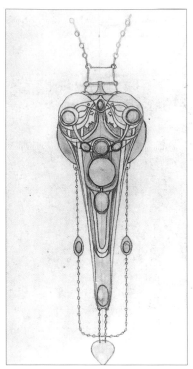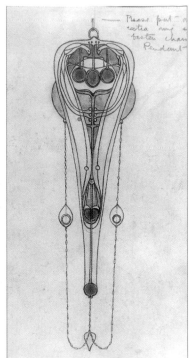

with which the schools of art were originally founded, viz., 'the practical applica-
tion of knowledge of ornamental art to
the improvement of manufactures.'" He
encouraged every aspect of teaching from
the start, brought his friend Aston Nicholas
with him from South Kensington to teach
design, and invited notable artists and craftsmen to lecture. On his arrival there were
nearly eight hundred students in totally
inadequate quarters. The poorer students
were trained as school teachers, relatively
well-off students, particularly young
women for whom it was a kind of finishing school, were charged fees, and the
evening classes were mostly for trainee
architects and artisans who were at work
or apprenticed during the day.

Some students were particularly noted
by Newberry. One of these was Jessie
Rowat (1864-1948) – a Paisley girl whose
father was a manufacturer of shawls – who
had originally intended to spend a year at
the School, improving her drawing. She
soon moved on to study painting and
anatomy, then textiles and stained glass. In

1886 she began to hold classes in enamels
and mosaics while also designing clothes
and embroidery, which she later taught. In
1889 she married Newberry, and they
were to have two daughters.

Another was Charles Rennie Mackintosh. Born in Glasgow in 1868, one of
eleven children of a superintendent of
police and his wife, his ambition was to
become an architect, and so he was articled at the age of sixteen to the firm of
John Hutchison while also enrolling as an
evening student at the Glasgow School of
Art. He completed his articles in 1889,
and joined the firm of Honeyman and
Keppie, Architects. He had won a number
of prizes for painting and architecture at
the School, and in 1890 he won the £60
Alexander (Greek) Thompson Travelling
Scholarship, which enabled him to explore
Italy. Some of the sketches he executed
during his grand tour were submitted to
the School's annual Art Students' Club
Exhibition in which he was awarded first
prize. Newberry, who liked to refer to
himself as Fra Newberry, noticed his work

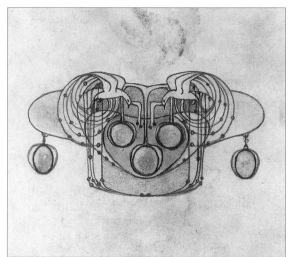

at this stage, and was henceforth to be his chief champion.

Mackintosh's closest friend at this time was Herbert MacNair (1868-1955). Born in Glasgow, he had quarrelled with his father, who wanted him to become an engineer, and had spent a year in Rouen in France, studying watercolour techniques. In 1888 he had apprenticed himself to John Honeyman, who was to take John Keppie as partner the following year. He also enrolled as an evening student at the Glasgow School of Art. Mackintosh and MacNair became inseparable, frequently going on sketching trips to architecturally interesting places.

Margaret and Frances Macdonald registered as day students at the Glasgow School of Art in 1890. Margaret (1864-1933) and her sister Frances Elizabeth (1873-1921) were both born in England, where their father was successively a colliery manager, an estate agent and a consulting engineer. He came from Glasgow, where his family had had a partnership in a law firm since the 1830s. Margaret and

Frances's older brother Charles studied law at the University of Glasgow, then entered the family firm. He was soon joined in Glasgow by the rest of his family. The work of the sisters at the School soon came to Fra Newberry's attention, and he saw a similarity of style and aims in their work and the work of Mackintosh and MacNair. They would have been unlikely to meet, as the men were evening students and the sisters day students, so Newberry brought them together, and they immediately took to each other, eventually becoming known as 'The Four'.

The work of The Four was curiously consistent. Their imagery was created with gaunt, almost skeletal human shapes in conjunction with highly stylised adaptations of plant forms. They were obviously aware of French and Belgian Symbolism, and the titles of their works were either sententious ('Time', 'Ill Omen', 'The Lovers') or programmatic ('The Birth and Death of the Winds', 'O Ye that Walk in Willowwood' or 'Girl in the East Wind with Ravens passing the Moon').

Jessie M. King, Two pendants and a brooch designed for Liberty & Co, silver and enamel (Victor and Gretha Arwas)

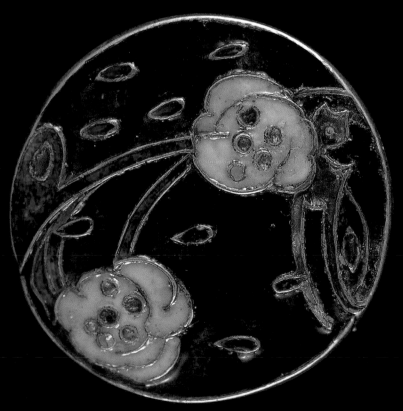

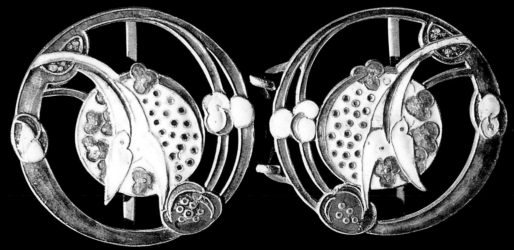

right:
Jessie M. King, Silver and enamel necklace using a bird motif also used by Archibald Knox

below:
Jessie M. King, Cloak clasp in silver and enamel using a floral motif and with a short chain to widen the space between the two sections

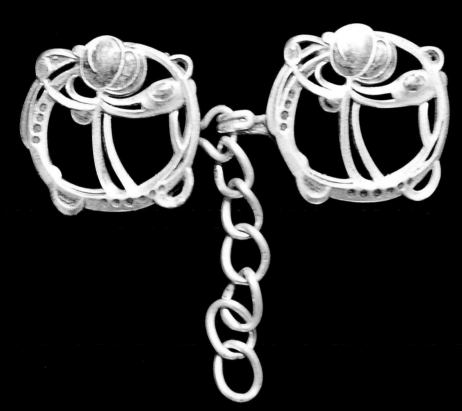

right:
Jessie M. King, Double circular belt buckle in silver and enamel with both flying birds and flower motifs in silver and enamel.

All three were designed for Liberty & Co. One half of either buckle or clasp was also retailed as a brooch

The Studio magazine had begun publication in 1893, reproducing the work of Aubrey Beardsley and, in the September 1893 issue, illustrating Jan Toorop's 'The Three Brides'. Toorop's adaptation of Indonesian stick puppets to create fluid 'human' imagery in which the flowing lines depict both the visual (cascades of hair, clothes, etc.) and the aural (the sound of wedding bells forming lines that echo and complement the visual) opened an exciting gateway into two-dimensional decorative schemes in which the Symbolist concept was made both more explicit and more vivid by the multiplicity of pattern and secondary themes which surrounded the main subject. Mackintosh painted several pictures in this style, but MacNair and the Macdonald sisters threw themselves fully into it. The style was derisively attacked as 'The Spook School', and many critics purported to see a decadent sickness there, the putrescent effluvium of diseased minds. In 1894 The Four exhibited at the Glasgow School of Art Club, but the local press was disdainful. *Quiz*, in

its issue of 15th November, pronounced: "As to the ghoul-like designs of the Misses Macdonald, they were simply hideous, and the less said about them the better."

Mackintosh was very much a rising star in his firm, and was given an increasingly large participation in the work. Part of the reason for this favourable treatment may have been his increasingly close friendship with John Keppie's sister Jessie (1868-1951), the youngest of five sisters. She, like Macintosh, was born in 1868, but was a day student at the Glasgow School of Art, where she won several lesser prizes. Mackintosh and Jessie eventually got engaged, and he made a repoussé brass casket for her. Though a member of the enlarged Mackintosh circle, she did not work in the style of The Four, although she exhibited a variety of objects along with them. In later years she was to concentrate on painting in watercolours.

The same opportunities were clearly not offered to MacNair, who was treated simply as a draughtsman. In 1895 MacNair left and set up his own office at 227 West

Jessie M. King, Pelleas et Melisande, *pen and ink drawing on vellum, 1901*

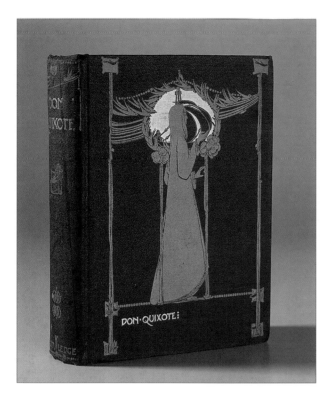

above:
Jessie M. King, Cover design
for publisher's book binding
for The Adventures of Don
Quixote de la Mancha

above right:
Clutha glass vase with internal swirls, design attributed
to Dr. Christopher Dresser

right:
E.A. Taylor, Two Red Roses
across the Moon, Water-
colour design for a stained
glass window

opposite:
Jessie M. King, His Dream, "He
would bring her acorn cuts
and dew drenched anemones
and tiny glow worms to be
stars in the pale gold of her
hair," Pen and ink, wash and
silver paint on vellum, signed,
an illustration for Oscar
Wilde's A House of Pome-
granates, 1915

HIS DREAM HE·WOVLD·BRING·HER·ACORN·CVPS·AND·DEW-
DRENCHED·ANEMONES·AND·TINY·GLOW-WORMS·
TO·BE·STARS·IN·THE·PALE·GOLD·OF·HER·HAIR

above:

Charles Rennie Mackintosh, A pair of oak armchairs for Miss Cranston's Willow Tea Rooms, c.1903. They were used in the Front and Back Saloons, the Gallery and the Smoking Rooms, placed at square tables for two to four persons

opposite:

Charles Rennie Mackintosh, Smoker's cabinet incorporating two repoussé copper panels in the doors by Margaret MacDonald Mackintosh. It was exhibited at the Secessionist Exhibition in Vienna in 1900 where it was sold, and Mackintosh had a second one executed for his own use

George Street, Glasgow. He had for years experimented with novel ideas for furniture, and he now put his ideas to the test, not only producing furniture but also designing bookplates, book illustrations, posters and stained glass windows as well as executing many drawings and watercolours. He frequently collaborated with the Macdonald sisters, who opened their own studio at 128 Hope Street the following year. Mackintosh in turn took a studio in Bath Street in which to carry out work independent of that at Honeyman and Keppie, as well as to hold regular parties for his friends.

Fra Newberry had organised an exhibition of work by his students at Liège in Belgium in 1895 following an invitation from the Secretary of L'Oeuvre Artistique of Liège, who had greatly admired the freedom Newberry gave his students thus enabling them to develop their individuality. This brought The Four some favourable notices, while Newberry's contacts with Belgium remained fairly strong. In 1901 he brought over Jean Delville, the

noted Belgian Symbolist painter, to supervise the painting school in Glasgow, a position he retained until 1905, when he was succeeded by Maurice Greiffenhagen, who remained Headmaster until 1929; he was elected a full member of the Royal Academy in London in 1922.

The year 1896 was a major turning point for The Four. The London-based Arts and Crafts Exhibition Society, which had successfully exhibited in Glasgow, invited The Four to exhibit in London. The Macdonald sisters exhibited two beaten metal panels, a beaten silver clock case and some posters, while Mackintosh exhibited a settle and a watercolour. The reactions of the critics and members of the Society were, on the whole, predictably unfavourable since their work did not conform to what was considered 'acceptable' by the blinkered arts and crafts heirs of William Morris. Only *The Studio* showed faith in them: "The Misses Macdonald show so much novelty and so much real sense of fine decoration in their works that a tendency to eccentricity may be

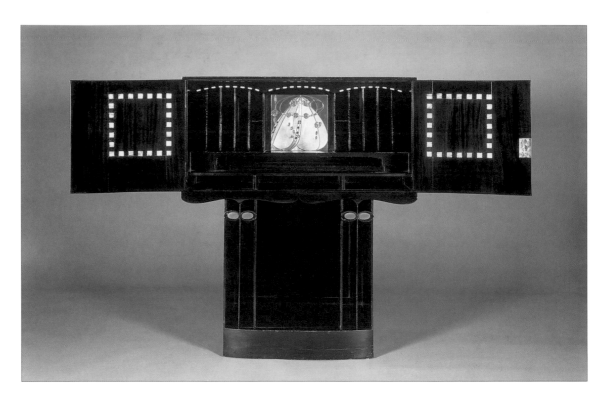

above right:
Charles Rennie Mackintosh, Writing desk of ebonised wood with inlays of mother of pearl, glass and metal, made for The Hill House, Helensburgh, 1904. A characteristic of this type of cabinet is that when the doors are open as here, the design is reminiscent of a Japanese kimono

right:
The same cabinet as above with its doors closed. Mackintosh later had a second cabinet with only minor variations made for his own use.

opposite:
Charles Rennie Mackintosh, Writing desk for the Blue Bedroom at Hous'hill, Nitshill, Glasgow, 1904. Made of stained oak with coloured glass panels and an inset panel of an abstracted weeping rose in leaded glass

easily pardoned. But this same tendency constitutes a very real danger; and those who are most eager in defending the posters ... and various subjects from their hand, should be also quite candid in owning that 'the spooky school' is a nickname not wholly unmerited. Can it be that the bogiest of bogie books by Hokusai has influenced their weird travesties of humanity? Or have the shades whence came the ghostly long-drawn figures, with pained faces and sadness passing words, afforded them special inspiration? ... Charles R. Mackintosh ... is obviously under the same influence ... One thing however is clear, that in their own way, unmoved by ridicule – or misconception, the Glasgow students have thought out a very fascinating scheme to puzzle, surprise, and please. Therefore it were more wise to wait, and if one does not grasp their plan, to give them the benefit of the doubt, and conclude that possibly the fault is divided between the artists and the critics, and that sometime hence when the sheer novelty no longer amazes, a set purpose

may reveal itself.

"For that these decorators already prove themselves able to make beautiful patterns, of good colour, and decoration that is really decoration, one may be grateful. Probably nothing in the gallery has provoked more decided censure than these various exhibits; and that fact alone should cause a thoughtful observer of art to pause before he joins the opponents ... If the said artists do not come very prominently forward as leaders of a school of design peculiarly their own, we shall be much mistaken. The probability would seem to be, that those who laugh at them today, will be eager to eulogise them a few years hence."

The year 1896 was also the year of the limited competition to build a new Glasgow School of Art. A suitable, though awkwardly placed, site and some money had been offered to the School's Governors the previous year, and a public appeal produced enough to consider building. Eight Glasgow firms of architects were invited to submit designs, though this number

right:
Charles Rennie Mackintosh,
The Hill House, Master
Bedroom, wide view from bed
alcove

below right: .
Charles Rennie Mackintosh,
The Mackintosh House, part
view of the Dining Room.
Mackintosh's white furniture
had been designed for his flat
at 120 Mains Street, Glasgow.
In 1906 he moved to a house
at 6 Florentine Terrace (now
renamed 78 South Park
Avenue), transferring his furni-
ture to the house. It was pur-
chased by William Davidson in
about 1919; on his death in
1945 Glasgow University
bought the house and
Davidson's sons presented the
University with most of the
furniture. When the new
Hunterian Gallery was built it
incorporated a re-creation of
the Mackintosh House, which
was demolished. The tall-
backed chair is a variant of
one for the Ingram Street Tea
Rooms, and is a delicate
extension of Art Nouveau. The
chair with the pure Art
Nouveau stencil patterned
canvas back is a variant of one
shown at the Turin
International Exhibition in
1902.

Opposite:
Charles Rennie Mackintosh,
Reconstruction of the
Mackintosh House Drawing
Room

 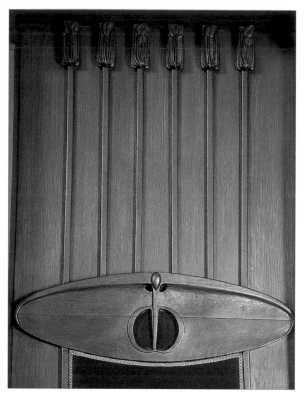

above:
Charles Rennie Mackintosh,
Detail of a bench end carved
with a Spook School face in
Craigie Hall, designed by
John Honeyman, later
altered by Keppie, for which
Mackintosh designed some
carved decorations and
leaded glass, 1893-94

above right:
Charles Rennie Mackintosh,
Detail of the carved oak pul-
pit at Queen's Cross Church,
Glasgow, 1899

right:
Charles Rennie Mackintosh,
Recreation of part of the
Dining Room of The Mackin-
tosh House

Charles Rennie Mackintosh,
Stained oak cabinet with a
stained glass panel and
inlaid with mother of pearl,
designed as one of a pair of
free-standing fitted bedside
cabinets for the Blue Bed-
room at Hous'hill, Nitshill,
Glasgow, 1904

above:
James Cromar Watt,
Enamelled gold pendant set
with opals

above right:
Mary Thew, Silver brooch set
with turquoise and other
coloured stones

right:
Glasgow Style copper wall
mirror inlaid with enamelled
panels

opposite:
Charles Rennie Mackintosh,
Oak washstand, the flat surface and back panel set with
ceramic tiles and leaded
glass, for the Blue Bedroom,
Hous'hill, Nitshill, Glasgow

opposite:
Margaret Macdonald
Mackintosh, The Legend of
the Blackthorns, pencil,
watercolour and gouache. It
was her last watercolour,
exhibited in March 1922, not
quite three months after her
sister's death, and may well
have been inspired by this.

above:
Margaret Macdonald
Mackintosh, Two plaster tiles

watercolours often framed in exquisitely matching frames in hammered pewter by the Macdonald sisters, who also designed and executed a variety of metalwork, including wall sconces. In 1899 MacNair married Frances. A year later Mackintosh married Margaret: Jessie Keppie was desolate, and never married.

Mackintosh was going through his most successful period. He was invited to exhibit in the 8th Exhibition of the Vienna Secession, was designing his first important dwelling for William Davidson, 'Windyhill', working on interiors and furniture for his and Margaret's new flat, designing furniture for Dunglass Castle and the interior of the Ingram Tea Rooms. A year later he entered the House of an Art Lover Competition which was highly praised in Germany and Austria, and the drawings for this were published in Darmstadt in 1902. Curiously enough, almost a century later, a version of this house has now been built in Glasgow, unfortunately not under the supervision of its designer, and so achieved with a number of compromises.

Mackintosh designed stands at the Glasgow International Exhibition in 1901 and, a year later, designed rooms complete with furniture with The Four at the International Exhibition of Modern Decorative Art in Turin. In 1903 he exhibited in Moscow and in Dresden, became a partner in the firm now called Honeyman, Keppie & Mackintosh in 1904, and was elected Fellow of the Royal Institute of British Architects in 1906. In the years that followed commissions began to dry up. A few additions to buildings he had already built, some work for the faithful Miss Cranston, the occasional alteration, could not compensate for the disappointments of losing out on new commissions. Disputes with Keppie led to his resignation from the firm, followed by years of wandering in London, Scotland and France, with minimal architectural work, and much devotion to painting landscapes and meticulous studies of flowers. He died in 1928 of cancer of the tongue.

Margaret provided support, inspiration and strength. She had a share in designing

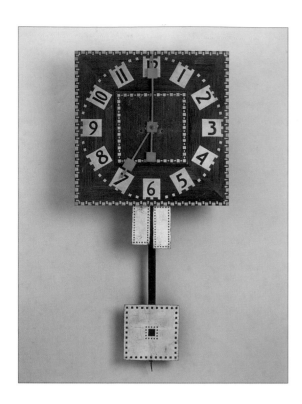

above:
Charles Rennie Mackintosh,
Wall Clock for William
Douglas; dark stained oak
with stencilled decoration on
face, weights and pendulum,
1910

right:
Margaret Gilmour,
Hammered tin clock, free
standing

opposite:
Charles Rennie Mackintosh,
Clock with ten columns
made for 78 Derngate,
Northampton; ebonised
wood inlaid with ivory and
green Erinoid, 1917

all his interiors, creating the gesso panels wearing white gloves and standing on a white carpet – clearly a very neat artist. Many of Mackintosh's later watercolours are signed with both their initials, though it is not known whether she had a hand in them. Certainly, in some of the major commissions, they worked side by side, each painting a decorative panel. He is known to have said, "I had the talent, Margaret had the genius." Whatever the truth of the matter, he was emotionally totally dependent on her, and miserable when she was away.

In an interview published in *The Connoisseur* in August 1973, Fra Newberry's daughter, Mrs Mary Sturrock, said, "My parents didn't like Art Nouveau and Mackintosh didn't like Art Nouveau. He liked simplicity and everything handmade. He fought against it with these straight lines against these things you can see yourself are like melted margarine or slightly deliquescent lard. Of course France was the worst. I sent two pieces of Mackintosh jewellry to *Les Sources d'Art*

Moderne exhibition in Paris in 1963, and was invited to the opening. They had a splendid room arranged by the Victoria and Albert Museum. They really had some very good Mackintosh stuff there, beautifully arranged, and then you went from that room into the French Arts and Crafts room which was oh, just appallingly bad. Glass and furniture, and metalwork and carpets. It couldn't have been worse. The lamps were melting, the glass was melting; well, you know the Metro signs, they even had them there, absolutely deliquescent."

Similar silly comments have been made by several writers, mostly people who see Mackintosh only as a precursor of the Modern Movement in architecture. He was certainly influential, and some of the designs of Adolph Loos in Vienna and Josef Hoffman's Palais Stoclet in Brussels in 1905 certainly owed a great deal to him. But what they miss is the fact that Mackintosh, like most of the great French and Belgian Art Nouveau designers hated and despised other people's Art Nouveau,

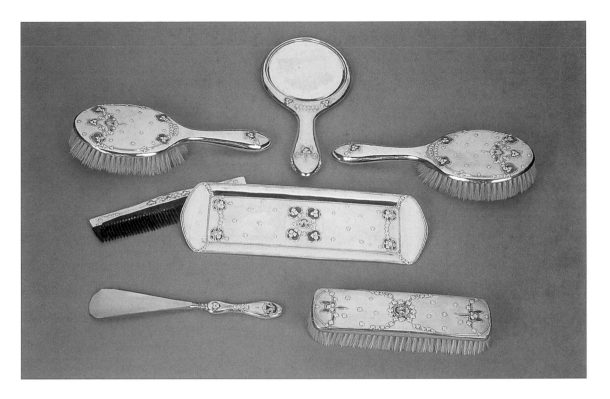

as each was busily creating his own vision which became his own version of an ever versatile style.

The decorative work of The Four forms the core of the Glasgow Style. Symbolism in various guises informs all their early watercolours and posters. While Mackintosh in later life concentrated on detailed and meticulous flower paintings and finely executed landscapes, Margaret Macdonald appears to have given up painting altogether in later years. The Macdonald sisters had, together, developed an ability to complete each other's work to present a seamless whole. They were able to paint or create three-dimensionally with identical ability, and while each was perfectly capable of creating on her own, each clearly sparked off and inspired the other. While Mackintosh occasionally joined in, and MacNair did at every opportunity, Mackintosh tended to draw and paint in a more solitary fashion. When they split up into pairs, the joint inspiration was sheared, each sister collaborating only with her husband.

Curiously, some of the sturdy individuality and creativeness of the sisters seemed to dissipate over the years as each subsumed her talent into her husband's projects. Mackintosh undoubtedly depended greatly on Margaret's magnificently spectacular imagery and great technical ability in most of his interiors. The couple exhibited at the Vienna Secession Exhibition in 1900, where they also showed pictures by Frances, who could not attend because she had just had a baby son, Sylvan. Gustav Klimt was clearly greatly impressed with the work of the sisters, which inspired part of the design for his great Beethoven frieze of 1902.

With most available commissions going to the Mackintoshes by 1900, the MacNairs moved to Liverpool, where he had been appointed instructor in Design at the School of Architecture & Applied Art at University College. He also carried out a few minor commissions, designing furniture, jewellry and silver, in all of which his wife assisted him; Frances also taught embroidery there. Together they designed

above:
Frances Macdonald MacNair,
A Paradox, *watercolour,*
c.1905

right:
Frances Macdonald MacNair,
Bows, Beads and Birds,
watercolour, c.1905

opposite:
Frances Macdonald MacNair,
Woman standing behind the
Sun, *pencil and watercolour,*
c.1912-15

FRANCES MacNAIR

Glasgow 55

background:
Frances Macdonald MacNair,
The Rose Child, watercolour
(detail)

opposite:
Frances Macdonald MacNair,
L'Esprit de la Rose, pencil
and watercolour, 1903. It
was exhibited at the Mir
Isskustva (The World of Art)
Exhibition in Moscow in
1903, organised by Grand
Duke Serge, who had been
very impressed by the work
of the Glasgow designers at
the 1902 International Exhibition of Decorative Art in
Turin. Mackintosh exhibited
a complete room in Moscow.

the writing-room for the Turin Exhibition in 1902. In 1905 the School closed but MacNair went on teaching at a local school and at the Sandon Studios Society, his minimal earnings supplemented by a small private income. This private income dried up three years later, and they were forced to return to Glasgow.

Although he had given up expecting any architectural work, MacNair could find nothing but odd jobs – he was, briefly, a postman – and the couple lived on Frances's wages as Assistant Instructress in embroidery and the Saturday morning classes at the Glasgow School of Art, where she also taught design in the enamelwork and metalwork classes. She continued painting and drawing, exhibiting at the John Baillie Gallery in London in 1911. Although several art magazines, including *The Studio*, illustrated her work, this did not lead to anything. Although the Mackintoshes helped out at first, they were clearly somewhat embarrassed by MacNair's lack of success, and their own problems caused them to leave Glasgow in

1914. In 1921 Frances died of a cerebral haemorrhage, although there were rumours that she had committed suicide. Devastated by her death, MacNair destroyed most of the works they had executed over the years and never returned to painting or design.

Talwin Morris (1865-1911), although not connected with the Glasgow School of Art, was a close friend of Fra Newberry and The Four, and was responsible for introducing Mackintosh to Walter W. Blackie for whom he designed The Hill House in Helensburgh. Born in Winchester, he was articled to an architect in Reading then in 1891 appointed sub-Art Editor of a new magazine, *Black & White*, which enabled him to work in graphics. In 1893 he moved to Scotland as Art Director of the publishing firm of Blackie & Sons. He designed many book covers, bookbindings and book illustrations, furniture, metalwork, jewellry and stained glass, decorated in pure Glasgow style.

Jessie Marion King (1875-1949) had a talent for drawing, and established a very successful career as book illustrator, with a

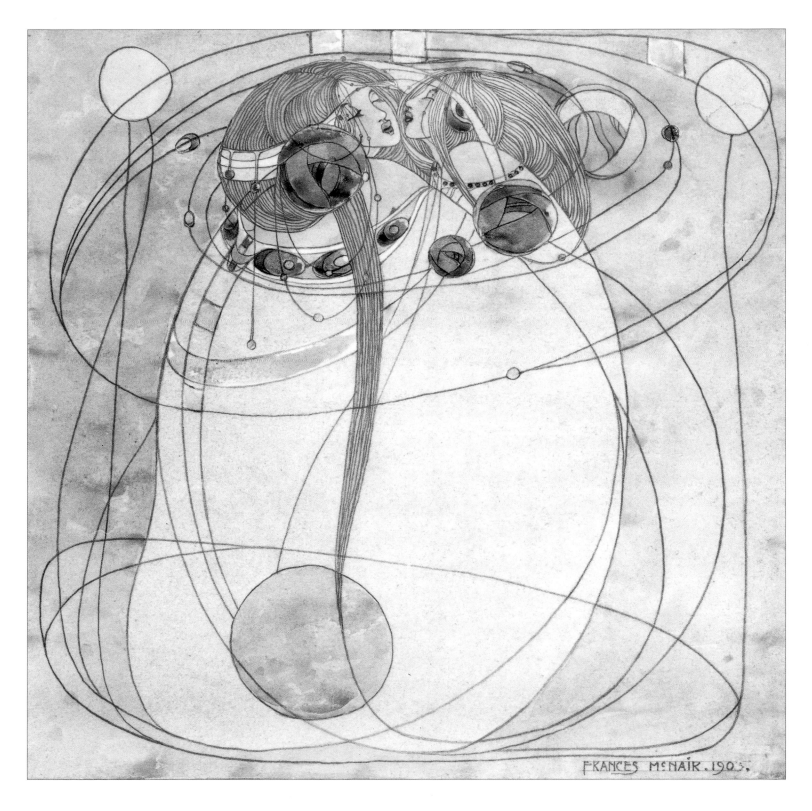

above:
*Margaret Macdonald
Mackintosh,* Titania, *pencil
and watercolour, 1909*

right:
*Charles Rennie Mackintosh,
Leaded glass panel, one of
four set into an oak toy chest
designed for William
Davidson's house Windyhill,
now in the Glasgow School
of Art. The rose motif,
abstracted in various ways
and in various materials, was
one he used frequently, and
was adopted by other
Glasgow artists.*

opposite:
*Charles Rennie Mackintosh,
Textile design,* Blue and Pink
Tobacco Flowers, *pencil and
watercolour*

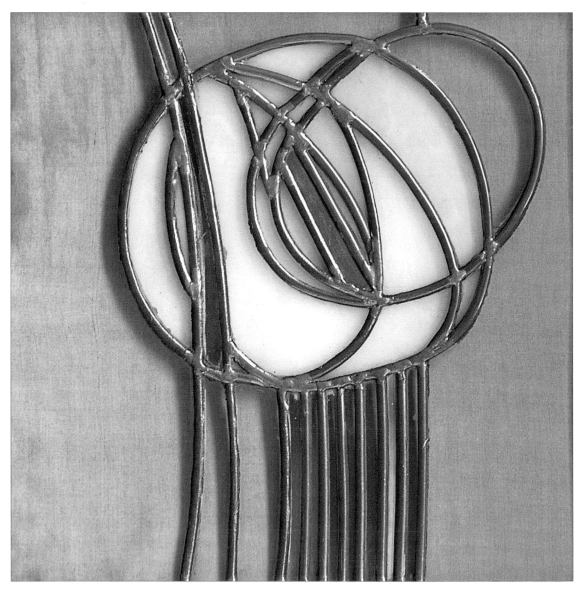

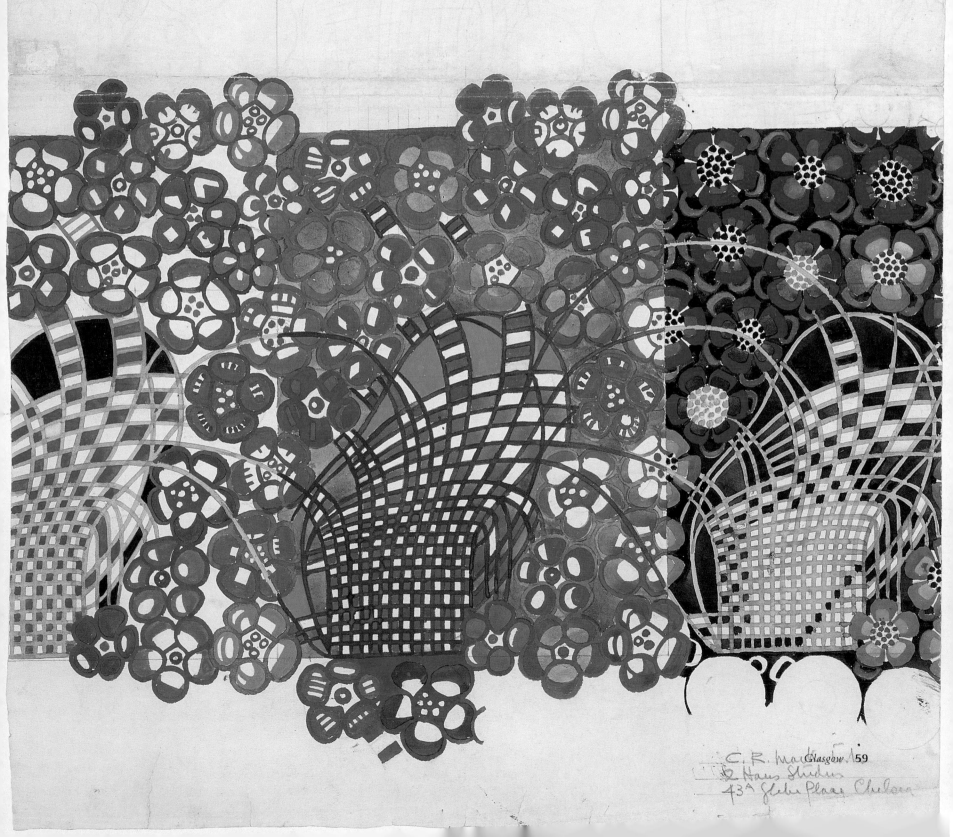

C. R. Mackintosh Glasgow 59
2 Haus Studios
43ª Glebe Place Chelsea

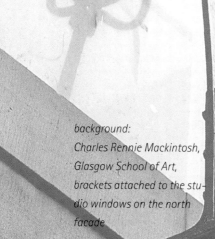

background:
Charles Rennie Mackintosh,
Glasgow School of Art,
brackets attached to the studio windows on the north
facade

opposite:
Charles Rennie Mackintosh,
Elaborate motif used as a
repeating pattern for a
stencilled mural decoration
for the Buchanan Street
Tea-Rooms, taken from his
watercolour Part Seen
Imagined Part, 1896

particular penchant for the Medieval, illustrating some seventy books, some of which she also wrote or compiled. She taught design for the bookbinding course at the Glasgow School of Art, herself designed a number of spectacular unique bindings as well as several publishers' bindings, and taught design for ceramic decoration for a year in 1907. Her eclecticism led her to design gesso panels, posters, toys, fabrics (she introduced batik to Scotland and wrote a book on the subject), wallpapers, bookplates and costumes for pageants. She also designed a range of silver and jewellry, mostly enamelled, as well as some items in gold and in platinum for Liberty & Co in London. She was awarded a Gold Medal at Turin for a book she exhibited there, and had her work exhibited in Cork, Berlin and Calcutta. She married E.A. Taylor in 1908, and late in life took to decorating small ceramic items.

Ernest Archibald Taylor (1874–1951) trained as a draughtsman at a Clyde ship-yard before joining the Glasgow firm of Wylie & Lochhead as a trainee designer while studying furniture design at the Glasgow and West of Scotland Technical College, and attending the School of Art part-time. He became part-time instructor in furniture design at the Technical College from 1900 to 1906 and Instructor and Lecturer in furniture design at the School of Art from 1903 to 1905. He, George Logan (1866-1939) and John Ednie (1876 -1934) designed furniture for Wylie & Lochhead in a sober Art Nouveau style which was acclaimed at the Glasgow International Exhibition in 1901, then at Turin in 1902, and in Budapest that same year. Logan designed furniture for Wylie & Lochhead until 1937 as well as for The Greenock Cabinetmaking Company (which executed several items of furniture for Mackintosh), and ran the furniture department at the Technical School with Taylor from 1899 to 1914. A screen he exhibited at Turin incorporated a panel by Jessie M. King. Taylor became designer and manager of George Wragge & Co. in Manchester from 1907 to 1911, and there

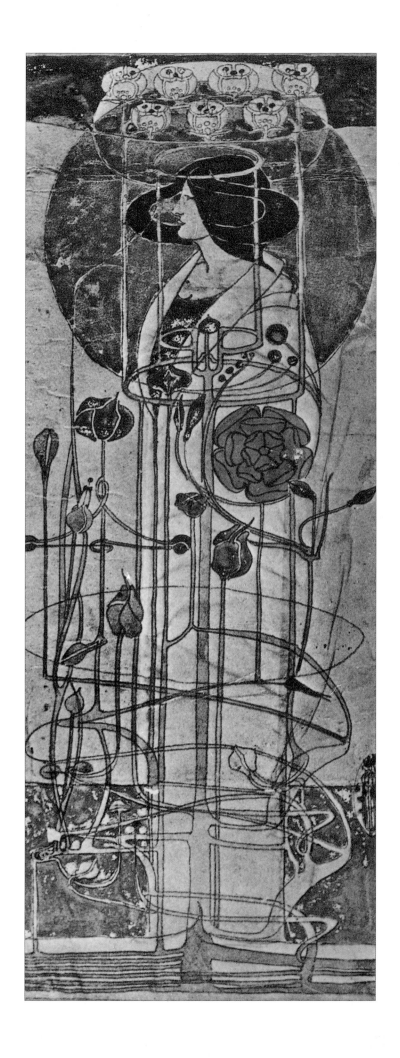

above:
Frances Macdonald MacNair,
The Moonlit Garden, *pencil*
with grey and white wash on
tracing paper, c.1892-98

right:
Frances Macdonald MacNair,
The Spirit of the Rose, *silk*
embroidery on linen,
c.1900-05

opposite:
Frances Macdonald MacNair,
The Rose Child, *pencil and*
watercolour

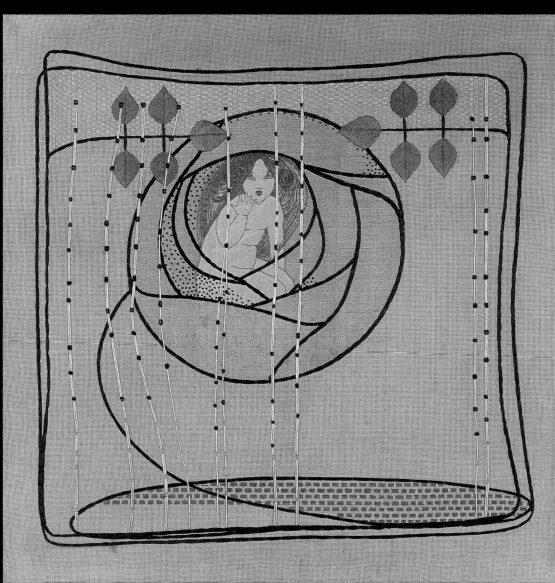

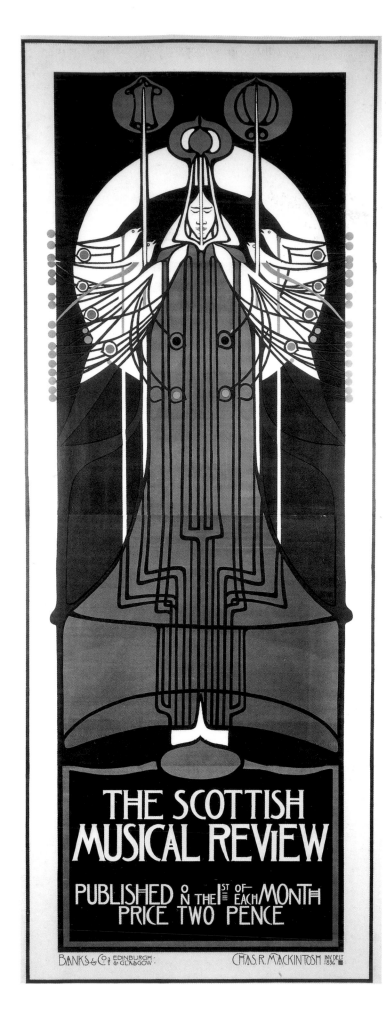

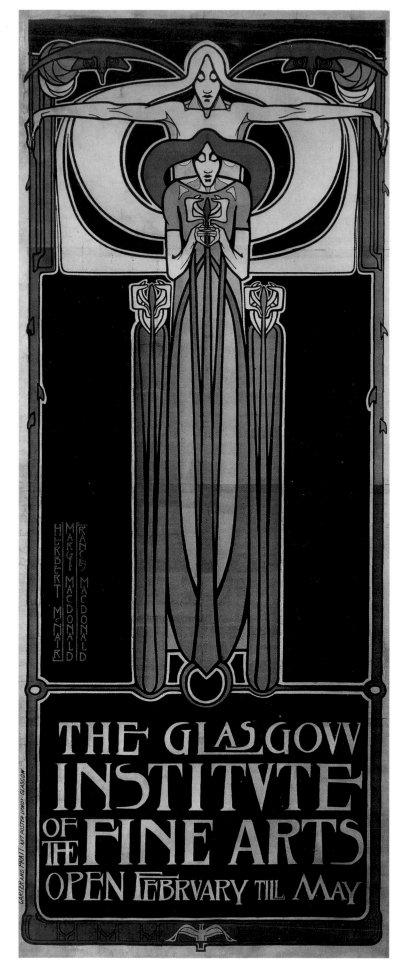

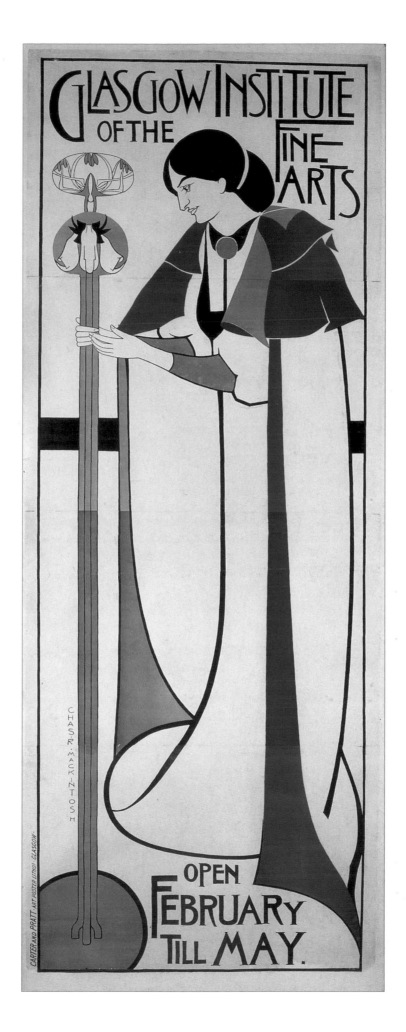

right:
Charles Rennie Mackintosh,
poster for The Glasgow
Institute of the Fine Arts,
colour lithograph, 1895

opposite left:
Charles Rennie Mackintosh,
poster for The Scottish
Musical Review, colour
lithograph, 1896

opposite right:
Herbert McNair, Margaret
Macdonald, and Frances
Macdonald, poster for The
Glasgow Institute of the Fine
Arts, colour lithograph,
c.1896

designed over a hundred stained glass windows. Jessie M. King also designed some stained glass panels. They both designed book covers, ran a sketching school, paint-ed, drew and taught applied decorative arts in Paris and in Scotland.

George Walton (1867-1933) attended classes at the Glasgow School of Art and, in 1888, received his first commission for stencil decoration for Miss Cranston's Argyle Street Tea Room, and later her Buchanan Street Tea Rooms, where he somewhat rashly employed Mackintosh to carry out the mural designs. Miss Cranston liked Mackintosh, and gave him increasing responsibility in the design of her various Tea Rooms. Walton designed many interiors, both domestic and commercial, including many shops for Kodak in Britain and abroad. In the late 1890s he succeeded Christopher Dresser as designer of 'Clutha' glass for James Couper & Sons, a Glasgow glass house which had developed a range of bubbled, streaked transparent or translucent coloured glass vessels, some internally decorated with swirls and flecks of aventurine and gold.

Many former students at the Glasgow School of Art became members of the Glasgow Society of Lady Artists, and taught and practised a wide variety of crafts, including ceramic painting, sgraffito, gesso, enamelling, jewellry, metalwork, embroidery, needlework, silver, bookbinding, leatherwork, book illustration, stained glass and woodcarving. Several of them, with some men too, joined the Scottish Guild of Handicrafts and, to a lesser extent, the Scottish Society of Art Workers.

DUNDEE

Although Glasgow was the creative
fount of Scotland in its creation of its
own variety of Art Nouveau, other
artists were working in their own little
niches throughout the country. Several
worked in Edinburgh. A small group
also worked in Dundee.

From 1895 to 1897 a magazine called
The Evergreen was published in
Edinburgh by Patrick Geddes, who was
at the time Professor of Biology at
University College, Dundee and
William Sharp, who wrote romantic and
Symbolist poetry and prose under the
name of "Fiona MacLeod". Though
only four issues were ever published, the
magazine printed essays on evolution
and the mystical aspects of life,
Symbolist poetry, and Symbolist illustra-
tions, some by Paul Sérusier and
Andrew Womrath, several by Charles H.
Mackie (1862-1920) and Robert Burns
(1869-1941), both of Edinburgh, and
John Duncan (1866-1945), George
Dutch Davidson (1879-1901) and Nellie
Baxter of Dundee.

Burns and Duncan delved deeply into
Scottish myths and folk tales, and were
very much involved in the Celtic revival.
They, along with Davidson, his mother,
David Foggie, Stewart Carmichael,
Nellie Baxter and Alec Grieve exhibited
at the Dundee Graphic Arts Association,
whose members encouraged and helped
them as they developed a graphic style
that was, to a great extent, Art Nouveau
in both subject and treatment.

THE ANNVNCIATION

LONDON

pages 72-73:
William Morris, Trent *fabric*

page 72:
Pickford Marriott, The
Annunciation, *oil on gesso,
inlaid with mother of pearl
and abalone shell, and gold
leaf, 1901-08*

page 73:
Pickford Marriott, The
Faithful Knight in Equal Field
subdues his Faithless Foe, *oil
on gesso, inlaid with mother
of pearl and abalone shell,
and gold leaf, c.1905*

opposite:
William Holman Hunt, The
Lady of Shalott, *Engraving by
J.D. Miller. The luminous
quality of the engraving
brings out the controlled wild-
ness of the Lady's hair, which
was to become a feature of
much Art Nouveau imagery.*

above right:
*Nelson and Edith Dawson,
Wrought steel casket, 1896*

The second half of the nineteenth century in Britain witnessed the rise of a number of architects in pursuit of a totality of artistic effect in all they designed. They believed that no detail was too small to merit thorough study, intensely creative solution and wholly detailed design executed under their close personal supervision. Much of this stemmed from the influence of Augustus Welby Northmore Pugin (1812-1852), who trained with his father, a French émigré, before working as an architectural draughtsman for John Nash. He became a leading exponent of the revival of the Gothic style, designed furniture and fittings for Windsor Castle, then worked closely with Sir Charles Barry in designing, decorating and furnishing the new Houses of Parliament in London. He also designed metalwork, including silver, glass and ceramics.

Shortly after Pugin's death the architects Philip Webb (1831-1915), Norman Shaw (1831-1912), and John Dando Sedding (1838-1891) emerged from George Edmund Street's architectural practice: Street was to design the Law Courts in the Strand and write two important books on Gothic architecture. William Morris (1834-1896) also spent some months there as an articled pupil. Norman Shaw in turn trained Sidney Barnsley and W.R. Lethaby (1857-1931), while Sedding trained Ernest Gimson and Ernest Barnsley.

William Morris had gone to Exeter College, Oxford, to study for the church. He developed a close friendship there with Edward Jones (1833-1898), later Burne-Jones, and both abandoned the idea of a life in the Church of England. He toyed with architecture before being influenced to become a painter by the example and enthusiasm of Dante Gabriel Rossetti, one of the founders of the Pre-Raphaelite Brotherhood. This ambition proved equally short-lived, and in 1861 he set up his own firm, Morris, Marshall, Faulkner & Co., Fine Art Workmen in Painting, Carving, Furniture and the Metals. The firm designed and made many stained glass panels, and a plethora

above left:
*Royal Doulton Chang Vase
by Charles J. Noke and
Harry Nixon*

above right:
*Moorcroft Florian Ware
Floral Vase, c.1900*

right:
*A. Dean, Decorated tube-
lined glazed earthenware
jardinière*

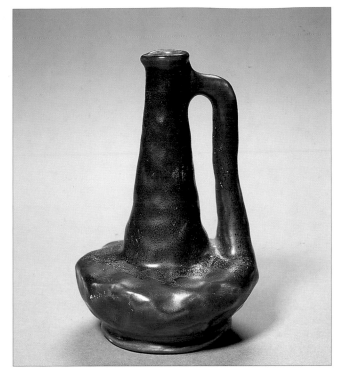

above:
Royal Doulton, Lactolian Ware vase designed by Robert Allen, 1899. Discovered by John Slater, this technique involved the use of coloured clays to achieve the designs, many of which were of Art Nouveau inspiration, and were exhibited at the Exposition Universelle of 1900 in Paris

above right:
Bretby Art Pottery, Glazed pottery ewer

right:
William de Morgan, Ceramic vase with a frieze of leaping stags

opposite above left:
top left: Silver cloak clasp set
with green cabochon cats'
eyes; top right: David &
Maurice Davis, silver cloak
clasp, 1901; centre: Joseph
William Taylor, Twin peacocks,
silver buckle set with cabo-
chon turquoises, gold crown,
Edinburgh, 1898; bottom left:
Guild of Handicrafts, Floral sil-
ver buckle, 1896; bottom right:
William Comyns, Lily pads sil-
ver buckle, 1900

opposite above right:
Sir Alfred Gilbert, necklace
made from twisted wire

opposite below:
The Wallpaper Manufacturers'
Company, Darwen, Three
Anaglypta Wallpapers with
relief decoration by G.C. Haité

of painted architectural tiles, later expanding into the production of wallpapers, tapestries, carpets, fabrics, embroidery, table glass and furniture. Philip Webb was chief designer of Morris furniture until about 1890 when he was succeeded by his architectural assistant George Washington Jack (1855-1932) who, though born on Long Island, New York, lived most of his life in England.

Burne-Jones proved the most popular designer of stained glass, while Morris designed several panels that were strongly medieval in feel; more were designed by Webb, Rossetti, Ford Madox Brown and others. Webb designed sturdy, rather cottagy furniture some of which was painted by Morris, while other pieces, such as a large cabinet designed by J.P. Seddon, which was covered with painted panels by Rossetti, Burne-Jones, Madox Brown and Morris depicting the honeymoon of King René of Anjou, were made to special order or for display on the firm's stands at exhibitions. But the most popular furniture consisted of sturdily constructed tra-

ditional items, such as the range of Sussex rush-seated chairs and settees, copied from an old chair found in Sussex in the 1860s by George Warrington Taylor, the Morris business manager.

In 1862 Morris designed the first of his forty-one wallpapers. Based on flowers, leaves, trellises and birds, the designs were highly intricate, the repeat patterns producing the illusion of an overall composition with no visible joins. Similar or identical patterns in various colourways on curtain and upholstery fabrics complemented the wallpapers, creating interiors which are the first full-blooded appearance of Art Nouveau in Britain. The use of floral ornamentation was hardly original; its treatment was. The repetition of motif was to be a characteristic of Art Nouveau in Britain, and the rejection of traditional Victorian stylisation in favour of an organic, flowing approach a component part.

The constrictions of early Pre-Raphaelite painting in Rossetti and Burne-Jones gave way in later years to

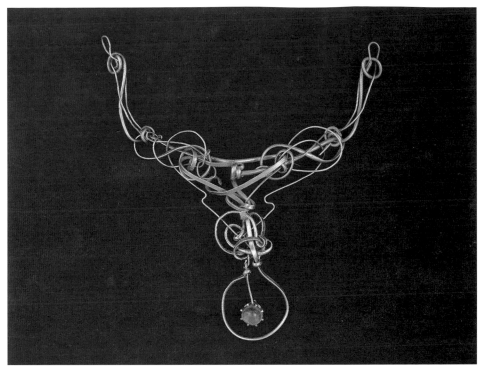

above left:
Liberty & Co, Oak high-back arm-
chair, the back made with spin-
dle-turned mushrabiyeh panel in
the Moorish style, de-signed by
Leonard F. Wyburd, c.1900

above right, clockwise from top
left: William de Morgan, Tile of a
crested bird of prey with a snake,
Sands End Pottery, c.1888-97;
Tile of the Bedford Park Daisy,
Sands End Pottery, c.1888-97;
Tile of a Great Curassow in ruby
lustre, Architectural Pottery,
c.1872-81; Tile of a Dodo in ruby
lustre on a white slip, Merton
Abbey, c.1882-88

right:
Armchair inlaid with a
Pre-Raphaelite maiden in mar-
quetry with mother of pearl

opposite:
J.S. Henry, Two chairs with Art
Nouveau motifs inlaid
in wood and metal, first exhibited
in the Dublin Museum in 1905

right:
Minton tile panel by Leon
Victor Solon, gilded and in its
original frame

opposite above:
Royal Doulton, At the Fair
Christening, *Lambeth tile
panel by Margaret E.
Thompson*

opposite below left:
E.A. Taylor, Kircudbright,
Stained glass panel

opposite below right:
Jessie M. King, Landscape
with Woodpecker and
Dragonfly, *stained glass
panel*

LIBERTY STYLE

 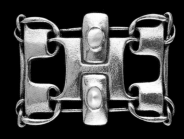

above left:
Liberty & Co, The Planta,
silver waist clasp depicting
honesty, designed by
Archibald Knox, 1903

above right:
Liberty & Co, Silver waist
clasp set with two blister
pearls, designed by Archibald
Knox, 1901

In 1875 Arthur Lasenby Liberty opened a store occupying half a shop at 218A Regent Street, a street considered the most elegant in London, and perhaps in all of Europe, designed by the architect John Nash as a continuously curved grand avenue of terraced buildings with shops at ground level surmounted at intervals by pedimented or terraced columns. Named East India House, this was to become the central fount of English Art Nouveau.

Born in Chesham, a small town in Buckinghamshire, Liberty was the son of a draper. When he was eight years old the family moved to Nottingham. Although he was a clever boy, he failed to win a scholarship, and since his father could not afford to pay for a university education, he was apprenticed in his uncle George's lace factory in Nottingham, and was then sent as a clerk to the wine warehouse of another uncle in the City of London. He did not like either job, but at the age of sixteen in 1859 became apprenticed to a Baker Street draper. This job at least gave him an opportunity to expand his intel-
lectual horizons by regularly visiting art galleries, museums, theatres and public libraries.

At the end of his apprenticeship two years later he went to work for Farmer & Rogers's Great Shawl and Cloak Emporium in Regent Street, a leading manufacturer of these fashionable garments and supplier of them to Queen Victoria and other members of the Royal Family.

In 1862 Japanese works of art were introduced to the great London public in an International Exhibition which also displayed Arts & Crafts objects from the Morris, Marshall & Faulkner Company founded the previous year by William Morris as well as a selection of paintings by members of the Pre-Raphaelite Brotherhood. Although a few avant-garde aesthetes in London and Paris had discovered the wonders of Japanese wood-block prints, netsuke, porcelain and other ceramics, bronzes and lacquerware this was the first time that a major collection, much of which had been assembled by Sir

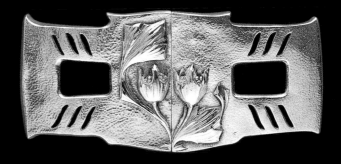

Rutherford Alcock the first British Minister accredited to Japan, was on public view. When the Exhibition ended, most of the collection was purchased by Farmer & Rogers, which put the items up for sale in a new Oriental Warehouse next door to the Emporium. Two men were sent to run the new store and Liberty, although the younger of the two, was named manager within two years. He quickly built up the business, attracting such fervent collectors as Dante Gabriel Rossetti, Albert Moore and Whistler, until, some ten years after he became manager, his department became the most profitable in the firm. At this point he asked for a partnership, was refused, and began making plans to set up in business on his own.

A brief early marriage to a young actress led to divorce, and his new fiancée, Emma Louise Blackmore, brought him a loan of £1,500 from her father, a Brook Street tailor who also guaranteed a further loan of £1,000 from a Bond Street tailor. Liberty's new shop opened with a staff

consisting of one of his former colleagues from Farmer & Rogers, a sixteen-year-old girl and a Japanese boy. He began importing silks from the East, and attracted all his former clients. Soon after Farmer & Rogers was forced to close down and Liberty was able to repay his start-up loans within a year.

Liberty began importing a variety of goods, including porcelain and other ceramics, fans, screens, wallpapers, swords, mats, lacquerware, paper lanterns, bronzes and wall masks from Japan. After the wearing of swords was banned in Japan in 1876 the metalworkers who had specialised in making swords and sword fittings for generations learned to diversify by making teapots, kettles and kitchen cutlery for the European market, much of it decorated with colourful cloisonné enamels, which greatly appealed to the English customers. In 1881 Liberty invested in a new Bond Street shop, the *Art Furnishers's Alliance,* which had been set up by Dr. Christopher Dresser and sold a mixture of items designed by Dresser and

Liberty & Co, Silver waist clasps showing variations in design or finish, all designed by Archibald Knox.
Top left: with central panel cut out; top right: central panel enamelled, 1901;
2nd row left: with floral enamel and set with two strips of abalone; right: with abstract enamel, 1903;
3rd row left: with central enamelled panels, 1902;
right: in plain silver, 1901;
bottom row left: in plain silver 1901; right: with enamelled panels, 1903

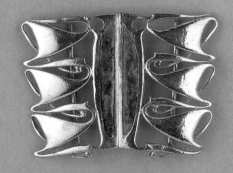

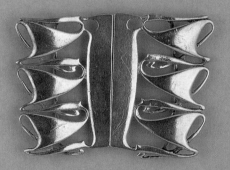

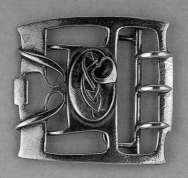

Liberty & Co, Waist clasps, all designed by Archibald Knox. Top: 1901; 2nd row: two versions of a buckle designed to commemorate the coronation of King Edward VII in the shape of the initials ER, left open and with enamelling on the edges, 1904; right: closed with enamel in the central reserves, 1905; 3rd row: with entrelacs, each with the prongs pointing in different directions, 1902 and 1901; bottom row left: with two additional leaves set with mother of pearl, 1904; right: in plain silver, 1906

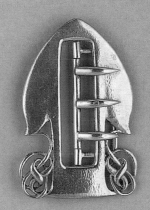

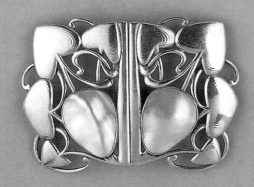

*Liberty & Co, Waist clasps in
silver designed by Archibald
Knox, four variations on the
use of the Celtic entrelac:
Top, 1900; centre, both 1900;
bottom, 1908*

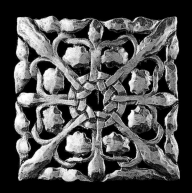

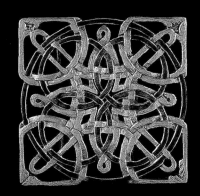

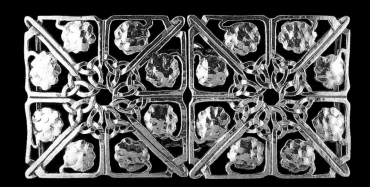

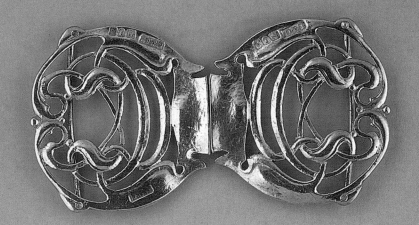

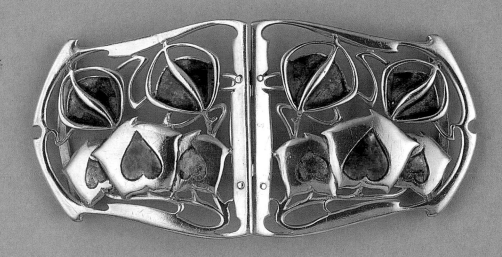

Liberty & Co, Waist clasps
designed by Archibald Knox.
Top: The Clymene, *1903;*
centre: 1903; bottom: 1902

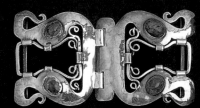

right:
Liberty & Co, Ten waist clasps
in silver set with coloured
stone cabochons, designed
by Oliver Baker

opposite above:
Liberty & Co, Pewter clock
with enamelled dial

opposite below:
Liberty & Co, The Magnus
silver and enamel clock
designed by Archibald Knox,
1902

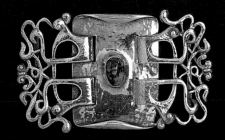

others imported from the Far East. Although the shop was forced into liquidation two years later, and Liberty lost his small investment, he undoubtedly purchased a fair amount of the stock from the Official Receiver at very favourable rates. Eighteen months after opening his shop he had taken over the second half of it; then, in 1883 he moved further south in Regent Street to a new and much larger shop, which he named Chesham House after his birthplace.

He began importing small items of furniture from North Africa, then offered through his catalogues a design service for bamboo furniture, which was described as 'Anglo-Indian' although it was actually designed by a Frenchman, Ursin Fortier, and made up in his workshop in Dean Street, Soho, very close to Liberty's shop. As the selling of furniture prospered, Fortier worked exclusively for Liberty, and the new designs were exhibited in the gallery of the Royal School of Needlework in South Kensington. In 1883 the furniture department was

above:
Liberty & Co, Silver and
enamel clock designed by
Archibald Knox, 1901

right:
Liberty & Co, Silver clock
with copper numerals, set
with mother of pearl
plaques and two lapis lazuli
cabochons designed by
Archibald Knox, 1903

opposite:
Liberty & Co, Silver clock
with enamel dial designed
by Archibald Knox, 1905

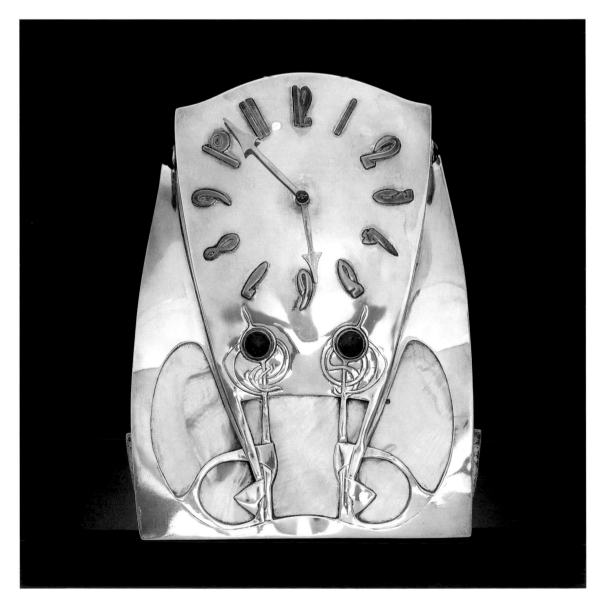

above left:
Liberty & Co, Silver and
enamel photo frame set
with mother of pearl and
moonstones, designed by
Archibald Knox, 1904

above right:
Liberty & Co, Pewter frame
designed by Archibald Knox,
c.1900-05

expanded into a Furnishing and Decorating Studio under the direction of Leonard F. Wyburd, who came from a family of painters. He designed a popular set of furniture which incorporated painted turned lattice work panels imported from Egypt and North Africa, where these panels, known as Mushrabiyeh, were used to screen windows and balconies, serving both to reduce the outside heat and to allow the ladies of the household to look out without being seen. These very decorative panels were used by Wyburd as chair backs and airy cabinet sides and doors. Inspired by Ancient Egypt, he also designed a three-legged stool with a concave seat, made of walnut, mahogany or oak, and a four-legged one with turned feet and an equally concave thonged leather seat. Named 'Thebes' stools, they were extremely popular and were stocked by S. Bing's Parisian gallery *L'Art Nouveau*. These stools were made from 1884 to about 1907.

Much of the furniture was traditional or roughly derivative from historical

designs, and was given fanciful names, such as Gothic, Saxon, Moorish or Saracenic, but towards the turn of the century, the firm also began to manufacture finely made items which are sometimes described as 'Edwardian' after King Edward VII who came to the throne in 1902 on the death of his mother Queen Victoria, but which are undoubtedly part of the nascent English Art Nouveau Movement. These items of furniture, often decorated with marquetry or mother of pearl inlays, were designed by such figures as C.F.A. Voysey, George Walton and E.A. Taylor.

The whole atmosphere of Liberty's was imbued with the concepts, influences and creations of the Aesthetic Movement. Tiles had become an essential aspect of home decoration, and were set into fireplace surrounds, the backs of hard chairs, as shelves on plant-pot stands, as wall decoration, as ceramic tiled pictures outside buildings, or inside hospitals, schools, pubs, banking halls or homes, or as framed individual tiles or sets of tiles

forming a continuous pattern. Mintons, Copeland and Maw were among the most prolific manufacturers, many tiles being decorated with pictorial patterns by Moyr Smith, Walter Crane, Henry Stacey Marks, Edward Hammond and Christopher Dresser. William De Morgan designed and made exquisitely coloured tiles of plants and flowers and fabulous or extinct birds and animals. At the turn of the century, and for some years thereafter, several firms produced tube-lined coloured tiles in Art Nouveau patterns, some inspired by Continental designs, but most by very Anglo-Scottish decorative patterns.

In 1871 Mintons opened an art pottery studio in South Kensington directed by the painter W.S. Coleman, in which professional artists, students and gifted amateurs were trained and provided with blank biscuit pottery, vases with flat sides, such as pilgrim-flasks, plates, plaques and tiles on which they could paint various subjects then fire them in kilns. These hand-painted tiles were, of course, differ-

ent from the commercial tiles which were normally transfer-printed. The Royal Doulton firm produced similar wares, called Lambeth Faïence, from 1873 when the Minton Art Pottery Studio burnt down.

Christopher Dresser's designs were everywhere in the Aesthetic Movement. He designed a vast number of items, small and large, for the Linthorpe Pottery in Middlesborough, adapting Classical, Anglo-Saxon, Celtic, Moorish and Pre-Columbian Peruvian shapes to a perceived Japanese ideal. He had, in fact, spent time in Japan in 1876, studying its art, bringing back artifacts for Mintons. Art pottery, different in design but within the Aesthetic Movement, was produced at Charles Hubert Brannam's Baron Pottery in Barnstaple, North Devon. Designed by Owen Davis or by Brannam himself, the Japanese-inspired pots were brightly painted and decorated in sgraffito. They were known as Barum Ware, Barum being the old Roman name for Barnstaple. They were stocked exclusively by the firm

right:
Liberty & Co, Two versions of
a silver frame designed by
Archibald Knox, 1906;
above: with enamel; below:
plain silver

opposite above left:
Liberty & Co, Silver frame
enamelled with a peacock in
his pride and peacock eyes
and feathers, 1899

opposite above right:
Liberty & Co, Silver frame
enamelled with stylised
flowers and leaves, 1901

opposite below left:
Liberty & Co, Silver and
enamel frame designed by
Archibald Knox, 1902

opposite below right:
Liberty & Co, Cymric silver
and enamel frame with two
enamelled copper doors on
copper hinges, 1900

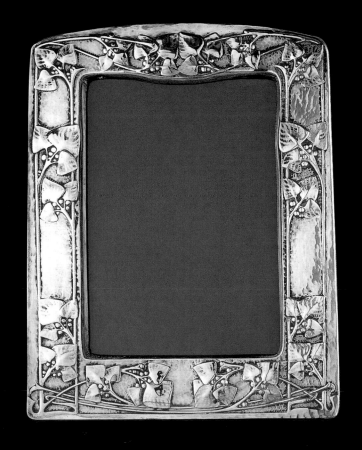

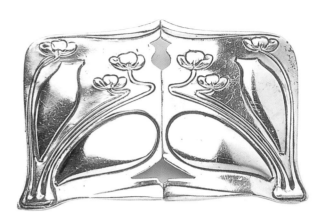

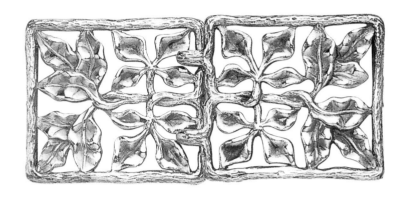

of Howell & James of Lower Regent Street. In 1889 a young Welshman named John Llewellyn left Howell & James and joined Liberty's, bringing with him the exclusive rights to sell Barum Ware. After H.B. Brannam died in 1937 his sons took over, and continued to supply Liberty's until just before the outbreak of the Second World War.

Liberty's stocked all these Aesthetic Movement ceramics, as well as the furniture, some cast-iron ware, and, of course, Clutha glass. Clutha was an old Scottish word meaning 'cloudy' and was applied to a type of glass which was bubbled and streaked throughout. It was made by the firm of James Couper & Sons in Glasgow to designs by Christopher Dresser, in free-form shapes, some of which were exquisitely beautiful, but were occasionally awkward and sometimes misshapen. The internal swirls were somewhat dull in the earliest ones, but once Liberty's decided to stock Clutha its influence was brought to bear on the glassworks, and the internal swirls became more intense and more

colourful. As Dresser reduced his work for Clutha, George Walton took over.

As adjoining shops emptied Liberty took them over and enlarged his shop until it occupied the entire block of 140 to 150 Regent Street. Of particular importance in the Aesthetic Movement was the availability of gorgeously coloured fabrics for which there seemed an endless demand. The Indian fabrics he imported were inconsistent in colour as the native dyes used were fugitive. He then began importing uncoloured fabrics, and arranged to have them dyed in England by William Morris's friend Thomas Wardle, a silk printer and dyer from Leek, who solved every problem as it came up. The range of colours and patterns, which were always given poetic and fanciful names, carried the name and reputation of Liberty across the world. The exotic beauty of Liberty silks led to the Art Nouveau movement in Italy being known as the Liberty Style, a compliment to both.

In addition to the importing of silks

and other fabrics, Liberty commissioned woven fabrics from a number of English firms, including Warner & Sons Ltd, Alexander Morton & Co, and J.C. Ward, and while it continued to farm out the dyeing and decorating of its designs to various firms, it block-printed some textiles and most scarf fabrics at its own Merton Abbey printworks, which were close to the Morris works.

Artists' models were frequently draped in Liberty silks when posing; the D'Oyley Carte Opera Company used Liberty silks and other fabrics for the costumes of their productions of Gilbert & Sullivan at the Savoy Theatre. Liberty was commissioned to decorate a room adjoining the Royal Box at the Theatre for the use of the Prince of Wales. Soon after other theatres, such as the Theatre Royal, Drury Lane, the Royal Opera House, Covent Garden, the Theatre Royal, Haymarket, and the Lyceum also gave Liberty similar commissions. When Gilbert & Sullivan's *The Mikado* was in rehearsal, Liberty sent out to Japan for just the right fashions and

Eight gold pendants with
enamel or mother of pearl,
designed by Archibald Knox,
c.1899–1903

top row:

Left: Carl Frey & Son, Silver buckle set with a central cabochon amethyst, two blister pearls and diamond chips, c.1905; right: Page, Keen & Page, Plymouth, Silver and enamel buckle, 1904

Second row:

Left: W.H. Haseler, Silver buckle, 1907; centre: A. & J. Zimmerman, Silver buckle in French Art Nouveau style, 1900; right: William Hutton & Son, Silver buckle designed by Kate Harris, 1904

Third row:

Centre: William Hutton & Sons, silver and enamel buckle designed by Kate Harris, 1899. This model was also made in plain silver and with inset mother of pearl plaques, right: William Hutton & Sons, Silver and enamel buckle set with coloured stone cabochons, 1903

Fourth row:

Left: Child & Child enamel-led silver buckle, 1902; centre: J.J., Silver and enamel buckle, 1908; right: Omar Ramsden and Alwyn Carr, silver and enamel buckle set with a tiny cabochon turquoise, c.1905.

Bottom row:

Left: Florence and Louisa Rimmington, Silver and enamel buckle, 1904; centre: Hukin and Heath, Silver and enamel buckle, 1902; right: Levi and Salaman, Silver and enamel buckle, 1904

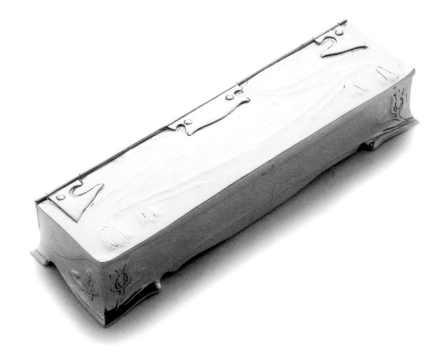

above left:
Tudric pewter box and lid
designed by Archibald Knox

above right:
Liberty & Co, Oblong
jewellery box repoussé with
stylised flowers

materials for the costumes and sets.

Boasting of a new fabric it was advertising in its 1883 Catalogue, Liberty's declared: "After many difficulties and a series of experiments, LIBERTY & CO. succeeded in inventing and bringing out the UMRITZA CASHMERE, which at once met with the most gratifying success, and has since steadily grown in favour. ... It is made in many neutral tints and all the art colours, and the long hairs scattered over its surface give it a very foreign appearance and add to its attractions. ... Furthermore, as imitation is judged the sincerest flattery, LIBERTY & CO. draw attention, with considerable pride, to the many subsequent and present attempts by other firms to copy their UMRITZA CASHMERE."

Liberty's inevitably attempted to build on its reputation for fabrics by also using them to make and sell clothing. These fabrics were designed in opposition to the uncomfortable, restrictive, unhealthy clothes which the fashions of the day dictated and which consisted of multiple lay-

ers of starched, stiff fabrics over a foundation of tightly-laced corsets stiffened with whalebone. In addition, since few women could afford vast quantities of changes of clothes, washing facilities were negligible, and so were washing habits, underclothes were worn for quite extended periods and outer clothes retained what would later be considered objectionable odours. The Rational Dress Society campaigned against restrictive clothing and encouraged the abandonment of the corset. Liberty fabrics supported this campaign, and were awarded a Silver Medal at the Rational Dress Exhibition at Kensington Town Hall in 1883. The following year Liberty's opened a dress department which employed the architect and designer E.W. Godwin as consultant and designer. He based the new clothes on ancient Greek models, loose and suspended from the shoulders, their effect based on "the exquisite play of light and line that one gets from rich and rippling folds." These clothes remained unchanged for many years, on offer through the catalogues, but were never

above:
Liberty & Co, Pewter butter dish with green glass liner by James Powell & Sons of Whitefriars, designed by Archibald Knox

right:
Liberty & Co, Pewter bowl with green glass liner by James Powell & Sons of Whitefriars, designed by Archibald Knox

right:
Liberty & Co, Hera furnishing fabric

below:
Liberty & Co: Three gold necklaces, left: with moonstone cabochons and baroque pearls; centre: with emeralds and pearls; right: with emeralds, mother of pearl and a pearl drop, all designed by Archibald Knox

opposite:
Liberty & Co, Three gold necklaces, left and centre: with mother of pearl; right: with abalone shell. All designed by Archibald Knox

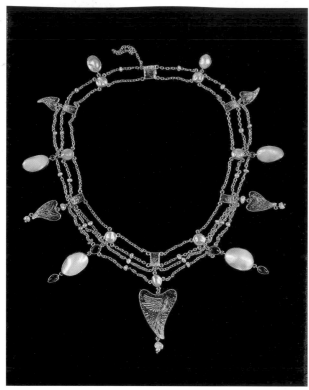

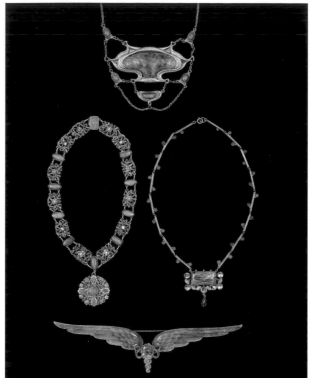

top left:
*James Cromar Watt, Gold
and enamel necklace set
with mother of pearl and
pearls*

top right:
*Ramsden and Carr, Silver and
enamel necklace; Arthur &
Georgina Gaskin, Silver and
enamel necklace set with
opals; Fred Partridge, Silver
and enamel necklace set
with moonstones and
chrysoprase; Child & Child,
Gold and enamel winged
intertwined snakes with an
amethyst*

right:
*Enamelled jewellery, oval
bottom right by William
Soper; bottom buckle by
Gertrude Smith; all others by
Nelson & Edith Dawson*

Royal Doulton - Chang
ceramic pot with lid
by Charles J. Noke and
Harry Nixon

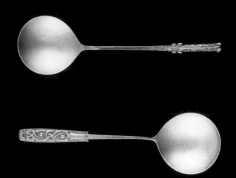

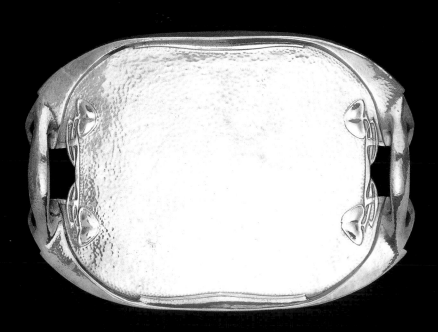

truly successful. Children's clothing, on the other hand, based on drawings by Kate Greenaway, was a runaway success, and was widely publicised with postcards and larger coloured prints, suitable for framing, which were to be found in many nurseries and children's rooms. Liberty fabrics, and particularly Liberty silks, continued to be the choice of the great couturiers in London, Paris, and indeed the rest of Europe and much of the world.

As the nineteenth century reached its final decades, the Aesthetic Movement gradually went out of fashion. The Century Guild, founded in 1882 by A.H. Mackmurdo, lasted until 1888. In 1883 the St. George's Art Society was founded while in 1884 it was the turn of the Art Workers' Guild. In 1888 were founded C.R. Ashbee's Guild and School of Handicraft as well as the Arts and Crafts Exhibition Society, after which the whole movement was named. The Society organised exhibitions in 1888, 1889, 1890, 1893, and 1896; the eleventh one, in 1916 as its influence was waning,

opposite left:
Liberty & Co, Pewter butter
knife designed by Archibald
Knox

opposite right:
Liberty & Co, Two large silver
serving spoons designed by
Archibald Knox

opposite centre:
Liberty & Co, Pewter tea tray
designed by Archibald Knox

opposite below:
Hammered pewter tea tray
designed by Archibald Knox

above:
Liberty & Co, Silver and
enamel cigarette case and
Vesta case designed by
Archibald Knox, 1909

right:
Pewter wall mirror designed
by Archibald Knox, c.1900

above:

Liberty & Co, Silver napkin rings, some with enamel, most designed by Archibald Knox, 1899 to 1907

right, from the top:
Liberty & Co, Silver and enamel preserve spoon, 1901; silver and enamel fruit spoon commemorating the coronation of King Edward VII, 1901; silver and enamel fruit spoon, 1901; silver and enamel preserve spoon commemorating the coronation of King Edward VII, 1901. All designed by Archibald Knox

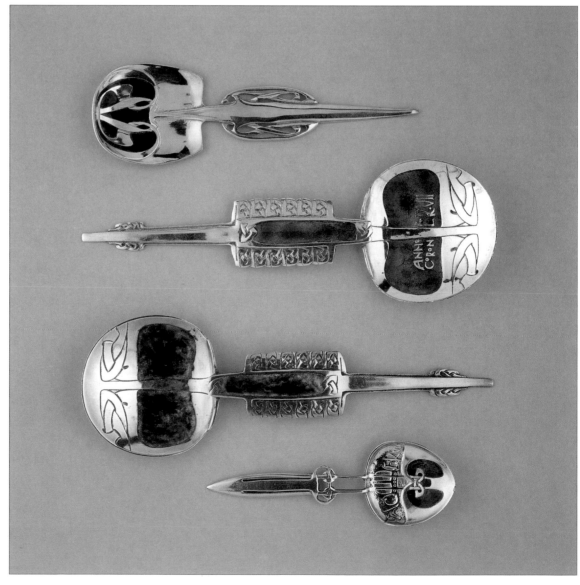

above:
Liberty & Co, Silver and
enamel bowl designed by
Archibald Knox, 1904

right:
Liberty & Co, Silver and
enamel spoons around a
button, most designed by
Archibald Knox

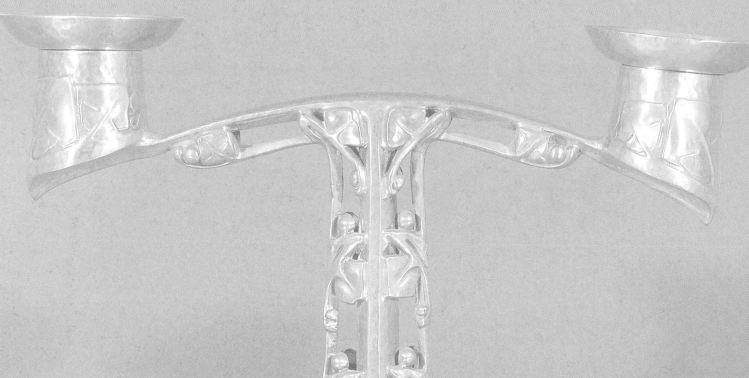

Liberty & Co, Pair of
double-branched pewter
candlesticks designed by
Archibald Knox

brought to the attention of the public not
only their new styles and ideals, but also
the names of several young designers,
many of whom were to design for Liberty.
The early, somewhat 'cottagy' look of furniture made by William Morris's company
changed in about 1890, when Philip
Webb left as chief designer and was succeeded by George Jack. Sir Edward Coley
Burne-Jones, a partner in Morris's company, and chief designer of leaded glass windows and panels as well as tapestries was
succeeded by Henry Holiday who also
designed stained glass for the Powell &
Sons Glassworks before opening his own
works in which he designed and executed
stained glass, mosaics, and enamels,
inventing a method of making shaped
enamels.

Liberty had been successfully importing
silver and pewter objects. Japanese sets of
spoons and other items were frequently
sold as wedding presents, and occasionally
given a Liberty hallmark; while the pewter
was mostly imported from Germany,
where Kayserzinn, produced by the firm

of J.P. Kayser und Sohn of Krefeld was
cautiously experimenting with Art
Nouveau designs among the more traditional ones. Other pewter manufacturers
whose products were imported and sold
by Liberty's included Walter Scherf & Co
of Nuremberg, under the name Osiris;
Mettalwaren-Fabrik Eduard Hück of
Lüdenshied; Rheinische Bronzegiserei of
Köln-Ehrenfeld, under the name Orivit;
and the Württembergische Mettalwaren-
fabrik, known as WMF.

Liberty's jewellery department had
opened in 1883, selling Oriental silverware and gold bangles, brooches and pendants set with precious and semi-precious
stones imported from India and Egypt,
China and Japan, as well as jades and
ambers. In the 1890s it began to import
jewellery from Greece and the Netherlands, and also began making small items
of jewellery in its own workrooms. Although most of these designs consisted of
pastiches of early designs, Liberty realised
that Celtic patterns were becoming
increasingly popular. The 'Tara' brooch,

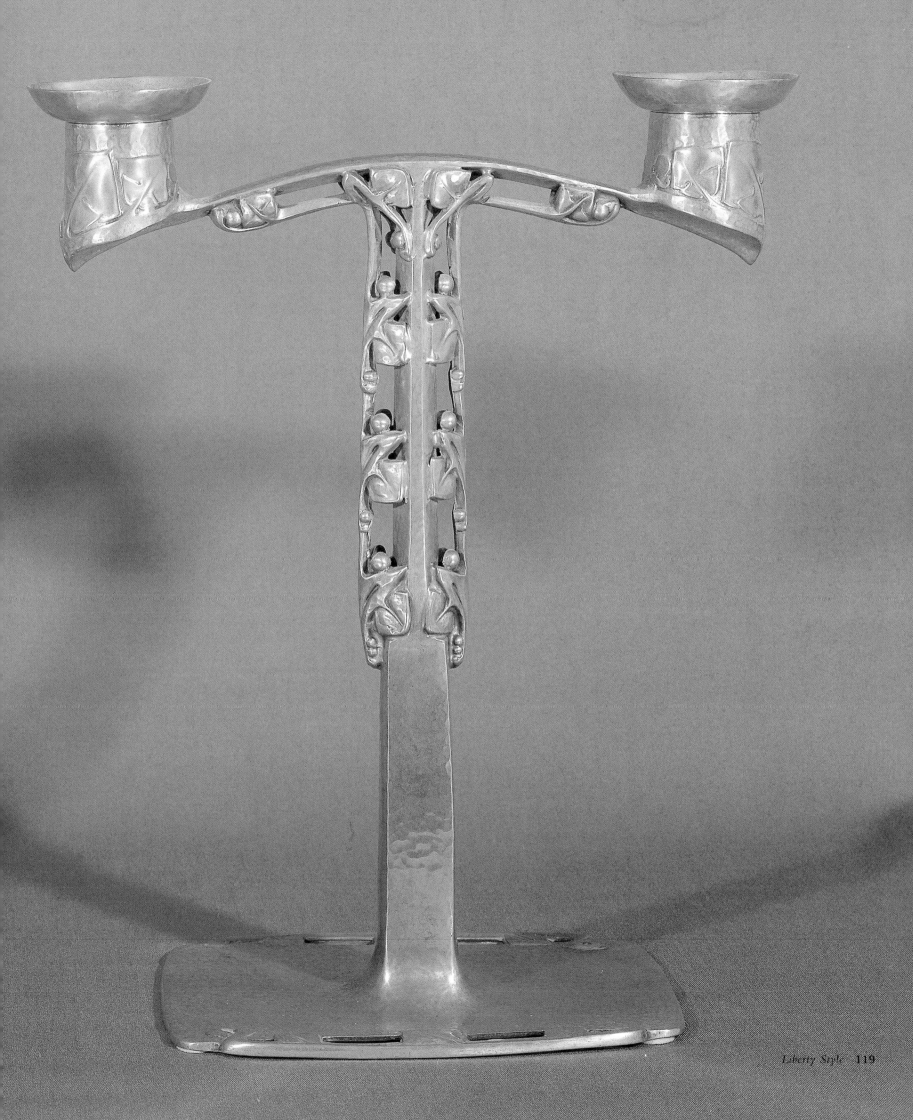

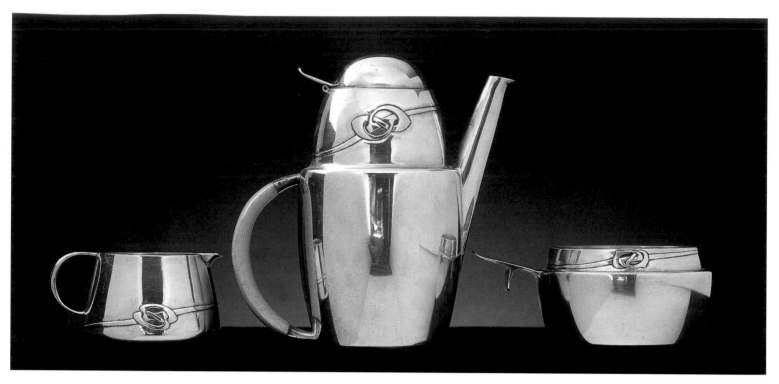

above:
Liberty & Co, Silver coffee set with ivory handle on coffee pot, designed by Archibald Knox, 1904

right:
Liberty & Co, Silver and enamel chocolate pot with cane handle designed by Archibald Knox

opposite above:
Liberty & Co, Silver tea set with chrysoprase cabochons, designed by Archibald Knox, 1901

opposite below left:
Liberty & Co, Hammered pewter bulb vase

opposite below centre:
Royal Worcester, Ceramic bulb vase decorated in Aesthetic Movement style

opposite below right:
Liberty & Co, Polished pewter bulb vase

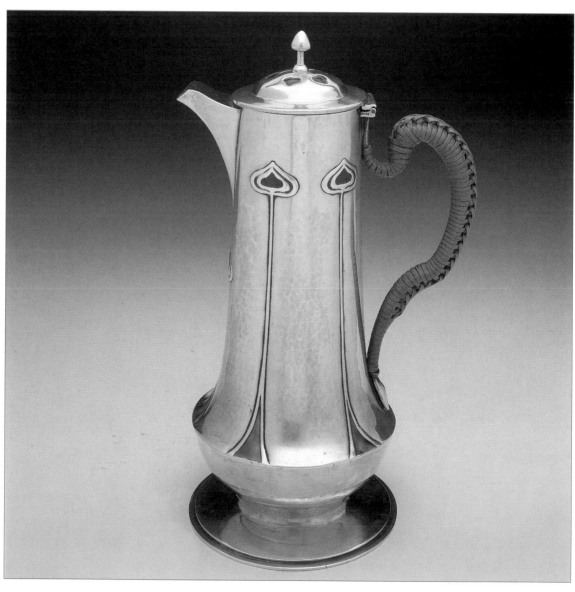

discovered in Ireland as long ago as 1850
had gone on exhibition all over Europe
and the United States, and finally entered
the newly-founded National Museum of
Ireland in 1890; a vast number of replicas
of this had been sold, two of which had
been bought by Queen Victoria. Other
artifacts popularised by replicas included
the Bell of the Shrine of St. Patrick, the
Ardagh Chalice and the Processional
Cross of Cong, while Owen Jones's
Grammar of Ornament and P.M.C. Ker-
mode's later *Manx Crosses* fuelled the
revival. Liberty had already commissioned
designs for fabrics and wallpapers from the
Silver Studio, and now ordered Celtic
revival jewellery and metalware.

Arthur Silver had set up the Studio in
1880, employing a number of designers to
supply many different manufacturers. One
of these designers, Archibald Knox, a
Manxman, proved to be the ideal man for
the purpose. Liberty's first Maker's Mark,
Ly & Co, had been registered as early as
1894 at Goldsmith's Hall in London for
use on some imported Japanese silver.

Several London silversmiths had been
employed to make up the store's designs,
but in 1901 a new company was set up,
Liberty & Co (Cymric) Ltd, whose directors were J.W. Howe and John Llewellyn
of Liberty & Co and William Rabone
Haseler and Frank Haseler from the
Birmingham firm of manufacturing goldsmiths and jewellers, and they were to
make most of the silver and jewellery.
The two Haseler brothers had inherited
the business from their father, William
Hair Haseler, when very young, and had
built up the business with a factory in
Birmingham and a London office in
Hatton Garden. This new company was
set up to formalise the agreement
between the two firms which had begun
in 1899 with the manufacture of silver by
Haselers under the name of 'Cymric'
(pronounced Koomrik) and in 1901 with
the manufacture of pewter ware, under
the name of 'Tudric'.

John Llewellyn, who had risen in the
firm and had just been appointed a member of the Board of Directors of Liberty,

above:
Liberty & Co, Two pewter
vases. left: set with water
opal cabochons; right: with
green glass inset by James
Powell & Sons of White-
friars, both designed by
Archibald Knox, 1902-05

right, from left to right:
Two Clutha glass vases
which were probably
retailed by Liberty & Co; a
Liberty & Co pewter holder
with a Clutha glass liner,
designed by Archibald Knox

opposite, from left to right:
Liberty & Co, Decanter
in pewter, designed by
Archibald Knox, and pewter
covered jug, both with green
glass liners by James Powell
& Sons of Whitefriars

right:
Liberty & Co, left: Silver and
enamel beaker; right: Silver
vase set with turquoise
cabochons, both designed
by Archibald Knox

opposite:
Liberty & Co, Pewter vase
designed by Archibald Knox

and whose family were shareholders, took control of the new metalwork venture, and had named the silver Cymric after the original Welsh name for Wales, and the pewter Tudric after the Welsh-born Royal Tudor dynasty. In 1899 Liberty registered two further Maker's Marks in Birmingham, *L & Co* in three conjoined diamonds, used from 1899 to 1927 with the assay office's date mark; and *LC & C Ld* in four conjoined circles, two up and two down, with the ampersand in the centre. This latter mark, intended for the new Cymric company was only ever used on a very few small items, and only in the 1893-94 year. All silver items for sale in Great Britain were normally fully hall-marked, but items for export often had only the CYMRIC trademark. Gold jewellery was normally completely unmarked, but most can be traced in a surviving Liberty Jewellery Designs index book. This is one of three volumes of outline sketches, Cymric silver, jewellery and Tudric pewter, each with its pattern number, assembled as a stock record by an

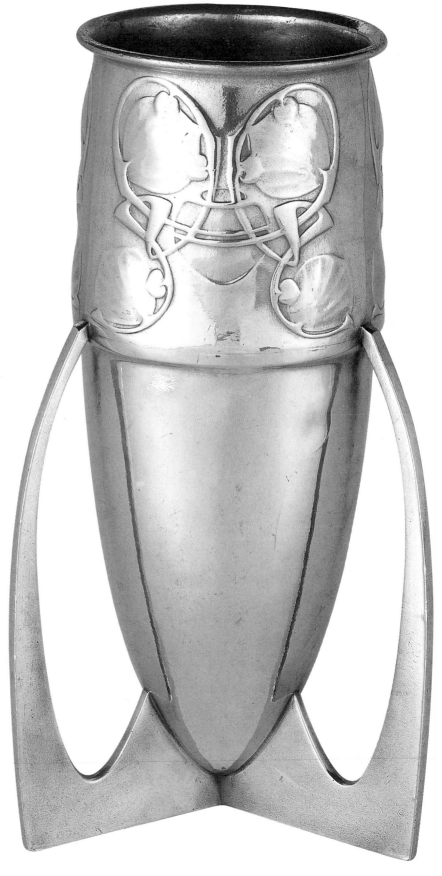

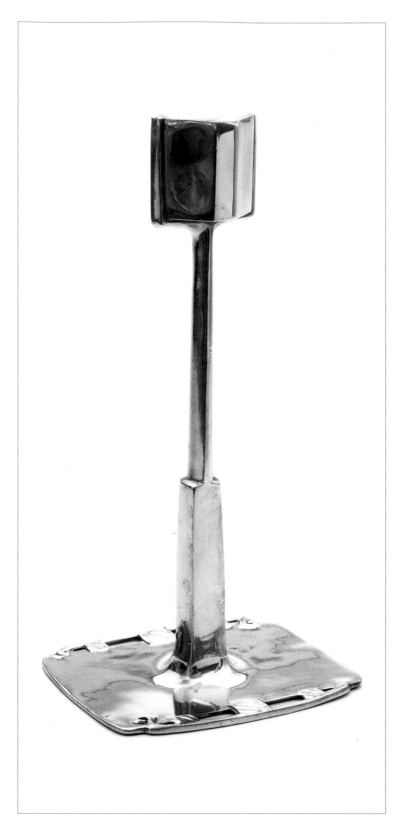

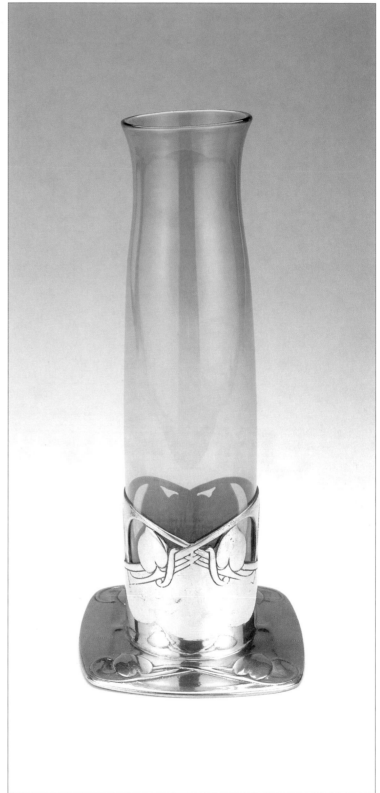

opposite left:
Liberty & Co, Pewter candle-stick

opposite right:
Liberty & Co, Pewter holder with green glass vase by James Powell & Sons of Whitefriars, designed by Archibald Knox

above:
Liberty & Co, Silver casket designed Oliver Baker, 1899

assistant and among the very few records to have survived.

Tudric pewter is found with a variety of marks, which can include 'Tudric', 'Made in England', 'Tudric Hand Wrought Pewter Liberty & Co', 'Made by Liberty & Co', or even just 'ENGLISH PEWTER', while some are marked with a Haseler sub-marque, 'Solkets' with crossed acorns above, which was a word made up from the firm's telegraphic address, a contraction of its original manufacture of *Sol*itaires and Loc*kets*. Although the lease of Haseler's premises and the ownership of its plants and tools had been taken over by Liberty, it continued to produce various works for its other customers, and marked a proportion of certain Liberty designs with its own Maker's Mark, *WHH*, items which it sold to some customers and also exported.

Cymric silver and jewellery was intended as a well-made, cheaper alternative to the very expensive Arts & Crafts hand-made products. Many short-cuts were taken to reduce costs, such as replacing the claw-setting of stones with inserting them into the surface from a hole in the back, then sealing the hole with a soldered silver pastille. Hollow-wares were spun or die-stamped flat then shaped, the resulting seam disguised with some hand finishing. Hammered (or martelé) decorative effects were occasionally really hammered, but more usually made by cutting facets into the surface of the die.

The great period of original Liberty designs in gold, silver and pewter objects and jewellery lasted from the late 1890s to about 1912, during which it established the look of English Art Nouveau as it was to be recognised many years later. Some designs went on being made into the 1920s and 1930s, while new designs in pewter and jewellery were much less original or elegant. The Cymric Company was dissolved in 1927, and Haseler took back its premises and tools, though they have continued to supply Liberty with goods. Tudric production ended in 1939, and most of the moulds were broken up and donated for the war effort. Liberty has

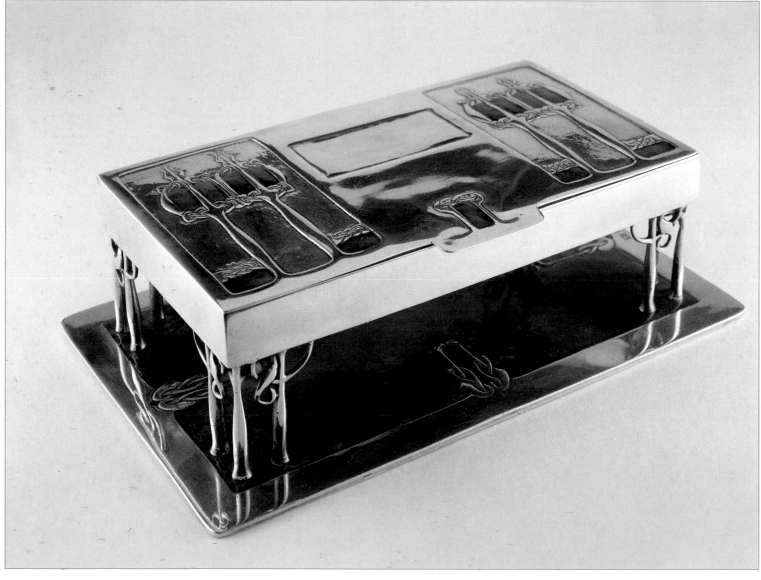

above left:
Liberty & Co, Silver chalice, the interlacing stems enclosing a top shaped serpentine stone, designed by Archibald Knox, 1903

above centre:
Liberty & Co, Silver and enamel chalice, designed by Archibald Knox, 1903

above right:
Liberty & Co, Silver and enamel chalice and cover, designed by Archibald Knox, 1900

right:
Liberty & Co, Copper wall mirror with relief entrelac and rivets, designed by Archibald Knox

opposite above:
Liberty & Co, Tudric pewter ice bucket, enamelled, designed by Archibald Knox

opposite below:
Liberty & Co, Cymric silver and enamel cigarette box designed by Archibald Knox, 1901

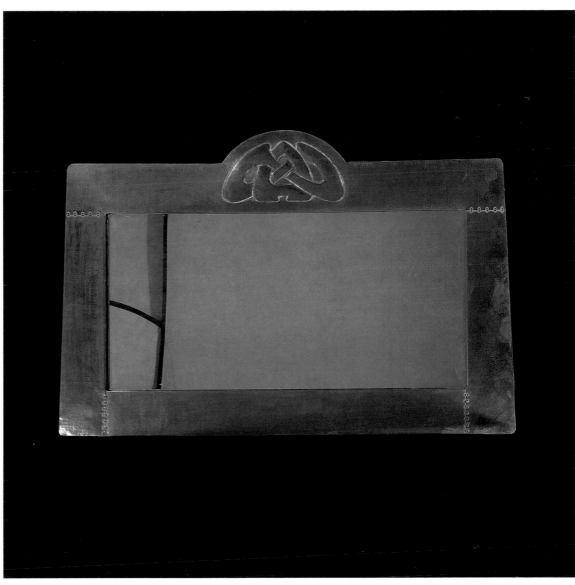

recently begun to reissue reproductions of a few of its Art Nouveau pewter designs, though these are not always identical to the originals.

Archibald Knox supplied Liberty with several hundred designs, while other members of the Silver Studio supplied others. Among the many great British designers who supplied Liberty with designs for silver, pewter and jewellery were Jessie M. King and her husband, E.A. Taylor, both members of Charles Rennie Mackintosh's circle in Glasgow; Arthur Gaskin, who became head of the Vittoria Street School of Art and Design in Birmingham in 1902, and his wife Georgina; Bernard Cuzner, Oliver Baker, A.H. Jones and H.C. Craythorn. Identifying the designer of an individual piece is not always possible, for Liberty made a point of never revealing the names of its designers, as only the Liberty name was meant to be publicised. While some pieces are known because they were either exhibited at an Arts & Crafts Society show where the names of the individual had to

be listed or had been illustrated in a foreign (particularly German) journal which named names, most other identifications are based on stylistic interpretation. Even here there are problems, as Liberty frequently adapted designs in its own workshops, adding or removing edges at the rim of vessels, producing silver and enamel items in different versions, polished smooth, hammered and with or without added enamel. Some vases and cups had piercings in their bodies into which were inserted translucent stones such as moonstones.

If, say, Knox had designed a vase decorated with an entrelac pattern on its side, that pattern could well show up on a brooch, a pendant, a napkin ring, or a button. It is possible that Knox himself may have designed the alternative items, but it is just as likely that these adaptations were made in the Liberty workshops without any need for permission, since once Liberty's had purchased a design, it was free to do as it liked with it.

The buckles (or cloak clasps) were par-

opposite above:
*Liberty & Co, Gold necklace
set with opals and pearls
with a baroque pearl drop*

opposite below:
*Liberty & Co, gold necklace
set with cabochon opals and
peridots with an opal drop
pendant, designed by
Archibald Knox*

right:
Liberty & Co, Mahogany occasional table with floral marquetry inlays, made for Liberty by William Birch of High Wycombe, 1900

opposite:
Liberty & Co, Mahogany inlaid display cabinet, c.1900

right:
Mahogany bureau-cabinet
with fall front, hinged doors
and four drawers, inset with
stained glass panels depict-
ing the Glasgow rose,
designed by E.A. Taylor

opposite:
Liberty & Co, Mahogany dis-
play cabinet with wood
marquetry and inlaid with
mother of pearl and abalone
shell, the brass drawer han-
dles with enamel plaques,
designed by E.A. Taylor

above:
Liberty & Co, Thebes No. 2
three-legged mahogany
stool, designed by
Leonard F. Wyburd, 1884

right:
Liberty & Co, Mahogany
hall seat, formerly in the
collection of Countess
Greffulje, c.1890

opposite:
Liberty & Co, The 'Celtic' oak
sideboard incorporating
electric light fixtures, the
metalwork designed by
Archibald Knox, c.1901

opposite:
Liberty & Co, Three-tier
Aesthetic Movement side
table in ebonised bamboo
set with three ceramic tiles

turers to Liberty. Moorcroft produced very colourful wares which were retailed through the store, while some designs were exclusively reserved for Liberty. Wardle turned out a few very popular models which were also exclusive to Liberty. Ruskin turned out a wide selection of coloured ceramics, from very fragile 'eggshell' to richly coloured high-fired pieces; it also supplied Liberty with small ceramic roundels and other shapes which were retailed as buttons and cufflinks, were set into copper mirrors, or were mounted in silver or pewter as brooches. Royal Doulton sold through Liberty, as did the Burmantofts, Farnham, Aller Vale and Della Robbia Potteries. Imported ceramics included many from the Gouda factory in the Netherlands, Zsolnay in Hungary, Max Läuger of Karlsruhe in Germany and Giuseppe Cantigalli of Florence in Italy.

Imported glass included spectacular iridescent glass from the Loetz Witwe works in then Austrian Bohemia: miniature bottles were filled with scent and sold sealed with round-headed corks. In the 1920s Liberty sold *pâte de verre* by Argy-Rousseau.

The sole exception Liberty made to their policy of anonymity of designers was in favour of Mary Watts, widow of the painter G.F. Watts, known as England's Michelangelo. In 1896 she had begun the designing and building of the Watts Chapel, dedicated to her husband's memory, and completed in four years the painting and gilding of the interior as a jewelled Symbolist ensemble. As soon as she had finished, she set up the Potters' Art Guild and executed a series of massive pots and jardinières, mostly with Celtic decoration, which were designed by Archibald Knox, Gertrude Jekyll, the great garden designer, Walter Smith and Mary Watts herself. Her Compton Pottery was advertised in the Liberty catalogues, and her designs were illustrated throughout the *Liberty Book of Garden Ornaments* in about 1902.

In the 1920s the elegant Nash buildings of Regent Street were mostly torn down and replaced by more commercial buildings. Liberty's East India House was rebuilt under the supervision of the London County Council, but was enlivened with a massive sculptural frieze 115 feet long above the central curved recess of the facade, designed by Edwin T. Hall and carved by Charles L.J. Doman and Thomas J. Clapperton, depicting the treasures of the world, carried on the backs of elephants and camels and in ships to Great Britain in the shape of a statue of Britannia. Above the frieze three figures appear to lean over the roof of the building, watching the sights below. In the rear of this building Liberty put up a mock-Tudor building in Great Marlborough Street, built with timber from old ships, with a similar interior built around three central courtyards, each four storeys high. Joining the two buildings is a wall at first floor level with a splendid clock which rings at intervals when the figure of St. George on horseback chases the dragon with his lance.

above:
Morris & Co, Silk wall hanging decorated with trees in blossom and tulips, designed by John Henry Dearle, c.1919-23

right:
Alexander Fisher, Rose Tree, embroiderd silk panel

above left:
*John Paul Cooper,
'Ouroboros,' gold necklace set
with moonstones, based on
the legend of the snake (or
worm) which swallows itself
thus forming the perfect circle of past and future, 1929*

above right:
*George Frampton, Gilded
silver and enamel jewel,
adaptable as brooch,
buckle or pendant, 1898*

right:
*Guild of Handicraft, Silver
and enamel necklace, set
with sections of turquoise
matrix, designed by Charles
Robert Ashbee, c.1900*

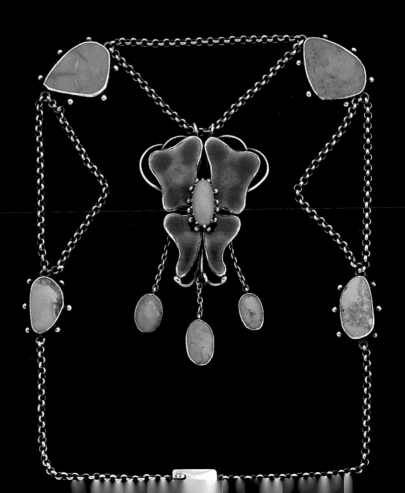

*Artificers' Guild, Silver
necklace with moonstones,
moss agates, garnets and
amethysits, design attributed
to Edward Spencer and
John Bonnor, c.1908*

Arthur and Georgina Gaskin,
Gold necklace set with
diamonds, opals, pink
tourmalines, emerald pastes
and pearls, c.1913

above:
Liberty & Co, Gold and pearl
necklace designed by Jessie
M. King, c.1900

right:
Artificers' Guild, Gold neck-
lace set with moonstone
cabochons, designed by
Edward Spencer, c.1905

above:
Fred Partridge, Silver and
enamel necklace, set with
mother of pearl, c.1900;
Nelson and Edith Dawson,
silver and enamel brooch,
c.1900

right:
Edgar Simpson, Silver necklace, the pendant enamelled
and set with chalcedony
cabochons, c.1903

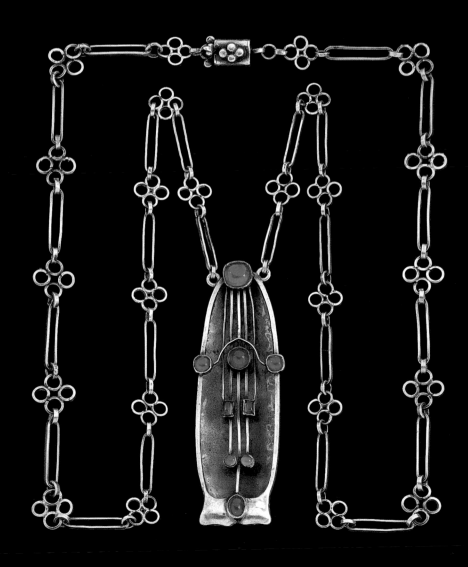

BIRMINGHAM

This provincial Northern city, steeped in commerce and the industrial revolution, somehow managed to foster an extremely active artistic life which impinged directly on London in general and on Liberty's in particular. Its heart was the Municipal School of Art in Margaret Street, which had attracted to its staff such creative figures as Arthur Gaskin, Sidney Meteyard, Bernard Sleigh, Henry Payne, Mary Newill and Charles March Gere through its headmaster, Edward R. Taylor. All around Birmingham artistic endeavours flourished.

Joseph Southall maintained a studio in Edgbaston where many Birmingham students came to study tempera painting. W. Howson Taylor (1876-1935), son of the School of Art's Headmaster, set up the Ruskin Pottery in 1898 with his father's help. Much experimentation led to the production of a variety of ceramics finishes and glazes, the most distinguished and spectacular of which were mottled high-fired flambé glazes in a variety of colours and textures. He sold his wares through

Liberty's, for whom he also produced small creations used as buttons, brooches and cufflinks and roundels used for insertion in mirrors and occasional furniture.

The Birmingham Guild of Handicrafts was established in 1890, developed from the Birmingham Kyrle Society, set up ten years earlier to encourage the working classes to "find enjoyment in something higher than the gin palace and more refined than the music hall." Gardening classes and the readings of plays were soon replaced by crafts classes and, by 1898, it was set up as a manufacturer of furniture and metalwork in copper, brass and silver, from table lamps and kettles to belt buckles and jewellery, from door furniture to other architectural metalwork. Similar work was produced by the Bromsgrove Guild which, however, specialised in complete house decoration, from furniture, metalwork and mosaics to decorative plasterwork and leadwork. The teachers at the School of Art all seem to have joined on occasion in the works of the Guilds. Joseph Hodel, one of the more interesting

J.J. Waugh, Cover design for Harmsworth Magazine, September 1900 issue, watercolour, 1900. Waugh succeeded in combining Art Nouveau floralism, swirls and lettering with fin de siècle Romanticism

metal workers at the Bromsgrove Guild, worked from London.

In 1887 the commercial manufacturers of silver and jewellery set themselves up as the Birmingham Jewellers' and Silver-smiths' Association, and it in turn founded the Vittoria Street School for Jewellers and Silversmiths in 1890. Set up to train workers for commercial manufacturing, the ideals of the Arts and Crafts Movement soon permeated throughout the School's teaching when Arthur Gaskin was appointed Headmaster.

The commercial firm of W.H. Haseler Ltd, run by W.R. Haseler, Secretary of the Birmingham Jewellers' and Siver-smiths' Association, and later its Chairman, who was also on the Committee super-vising the Vittoria Street School, sought a sales outlet in London in addition to its own Hatton Gardens offices. W.R. Haseler approached his brother-in-law Oliver Baker (1856-1936), an antique collector and historian, to design a range of silverware. Recognising his own lack of practical knowledge, Baker enrolled, aged 42, at

the School of Art and soon designed an original line of metalwork. Haseler took Baker's designs to London, showed them to John Llewellyn who in turn took them to Liberty who liked them, took them for sale, and made a deal with Haseler's which led to the formation of their joint compa-ny. Baker designed silver, pewter, buckles and jewellery for Liberty, as did such pupils and teachers from the School as A.H. Jones, Bernard Cuzner and Arthur Gaskin (with his wife Georgie Cave France).

Albert Edward Jones (1879-1954) came from a metalworking family in Birming-ham, and went through a thorough apprenticeship before joining the Birming-ham Guild of Handicraft. He set up his own business, A.E. Jones Ltd, in 1902, making his own tools and adhering to the principles of the Arts and Crafts Society, with which he exhibited his own designs, though Bernard Cuzner and W.W. Gilbert designed jewellery for him. He also exe-cuted some designs by members of the Birmingham Guild and some by Ashbee, but his was an otherwise commercial firm.

right:
John Riley Wilmer, Perseus showing the head of Medusa to the cowering Dardanians, *watercolour and gouache, 1906*

below:
F. Hamilton Jackson, Towards Infinity, *watercolour, 1901*

Arthur Rackham, Brünnhilde on Grane leaps on to the funeral pyre of Siegfried, *watercolour and gouache, executed as an illustration for Wagner's* The Ring of the Nibelungs, *1911*

above left:
Ruskin, High-fired flambé glaze ceramic vase on similar stand.

above right:
Myra Shaw, Painted ceramic plaque of a witch on her broomstick, 1903; in a silver frame, 1905

right:
Foley Potteries (Wileman & Co), St. Cecilia Vase, painted underglaze pottery of Intarsio Ware, devised by Frederick Rhead in about 1897. St. Cecilia is the Patron Saint of Music

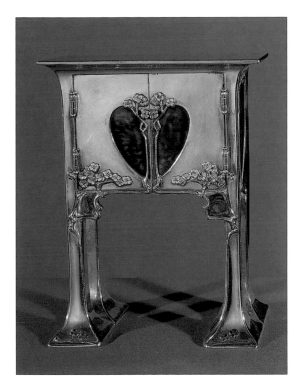

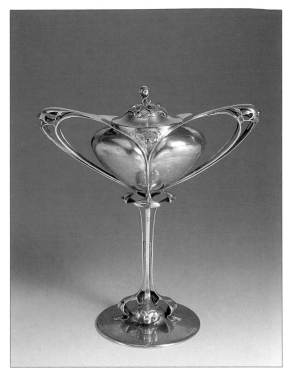

above left:
*William Hutton & Sons, Silver
and enamel reliquary set
with abalone shell, enclosing
a miniature portrait of King
Edward VII, 1902*

above right:
*William Hutton & Sons, Two-
handled silver cup and cover
set with fire opals*

right:
*Percy Gleaner, Burslem,
Circular polychrome ceramic
plaque*

above left:
William Arthur Smith
Benson, Copper and brass
kettle on stand

above right:
Bernard Moore, Ceramic
claret jug, mounted in silver
by the Duchess of
Sutherland's Cripples Build,
1907

right:
Minton tile, Autumn comes
jovial on by Moyr Smith,
1874

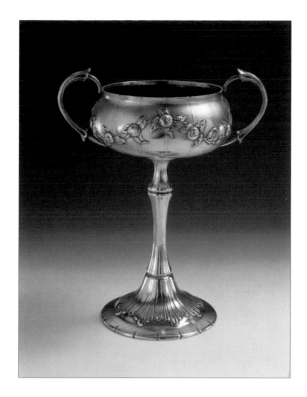

above left:
Gilbert Marks, Silver gilt two-handled tazza

above right:
Johnson, Walker and Tolhurst, Two-handled silver tazza on stand, designed by Gilbert Marks, 1904

right:
Minton tile, Flute player, by Moyr Smith, 1876

above left:
Florence Steele, Wrought
silver triumphal figure,
c.1900

above right:
Francis Higgins & Son,
Massive wrought silver
spoon, the handle in the
shape of a nude adolescent
boy, 1890

right:
William Hutton & Sons, Silver
picture frame with leaves,
plums and tendrils in high
relief on an enamelled
ground, 1902

above:
*Guild of Handicrafts,
Two-handled bowl, cover
and spoon, designed by
C.R. Ashbee*

background:
*Silver two-handled cup and
cover with opal matrix
cabochons, designed and
made by Gilbert Marks, 1900*

In complete contrast the commercial firm of Charles Horner turned out a very successful range of Liberty Style Art Nouveau jewellery, brooches, pendants, bracelets and necklaces in nine carat gold and diestamped silver with some enamel, mostly assayed in Chester, sold cheaply and now beginning to be collected. A native of Halifax, Yorkshire, Horner invented the 'Dorcas' thimble in about 1885, whose success enabled the firm to flourish. On his death in 1896 two of his six sons, James Dobson Horner and C. Harry Horner took over the firm, built a new factory and turned it into a limited liability company in 1909.

above:
Silver milk jug, the lid set
with a green enamelled
cabochon finial, ivory handle

right:
A.E. Jones, Silver and copper
casket set with Ruskin
plaques, 1902

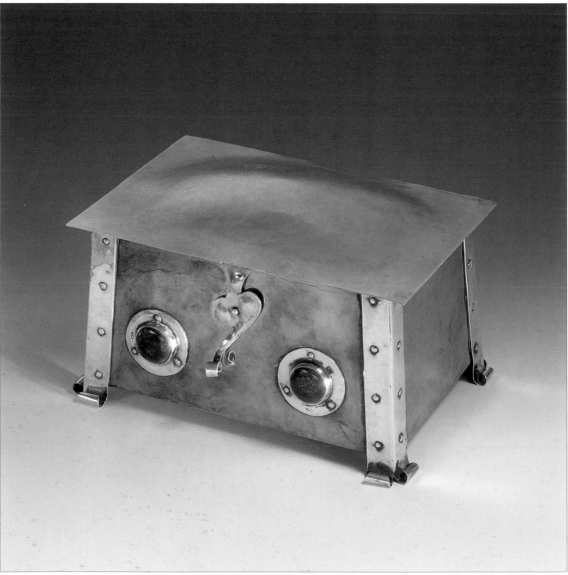

C.F.A Voysey, Cast aluminium clock with enamelled dial, the numbers replaced with Tempus Fugit, c.1920

ENAMELS

Enamelled jewellery of the Arts and Crafts Movement was most often *cloisonné*: the various colours were separated by fine wires, known as *cloisons*, which shaped the outlines of the desired image and were soldered to the surface to be decorated. The molten enamel was then poured into the cells formed by the cloisons; on cooling it vitrified into a rich hard surface. Although enamelling had largely died out in the early part of the nineteenth century, it was revived in France by Barbedienne, and Thesmar who worked for that firm, and was commercially revived in a small way by the Birmingham firm of silversmiths and pioneers of electro-plating, Elkington; but they abandoned its use in about 1879 when faced with large imports of cheaper cloisonné enamels from Japan and China.

Alexander Fisher (1864–1936), a scholarship student in South Kensington, travelled to Rome then to France, where a lecture given by Adrien Dalpayrat aroused his interest in enamelling, which he studied in Paris. On his return he set up a

opposite above:
Sir Hubert Herkomer,
Day, *enamel on copper,*
in a wrought copper frame
by the artist, 1898

opposite below:
Sir Hubert Herkomer,
Evening, *enamel on copper,*
in a wrought copper frame
by the artist, 1898

above:
Wrought and enamelled
casket

workshop where he worked as a sculptor and designer, but also as an enameller, specialising in so-called Limoges enamelling, in which pictures are painted directly on a metal surface with coloured enamel powders mixed with a liquid base, without separation of colours and so without the use of cloisons, after which the picture is baked and the enamel vitrifies into a jewelled painting. Fisher proved a master of the technique, wrote a number of articles on it which he later assembled as a book: *The Art of Enamelling on Metal*.

In 1896 he became Head of the Enamel Workshop at the Central School of Arts and Crafts in London, exhibited widely, and was awarded a Diploma of Honour at Budapest in 1902 and Gold and Silver Medals at the International Art Exhibition in Barcelona in 1907. He wrote: "Let us then start by thinking of enamels as creations, not copies, made as it were of precious stones, only with this difference – that instead of a narrow range, they are capable of an infinite variety of colouration." Paradoxically, faced

with that infinite variety of rich and dazzling colouration, he often chose to work in a very limited palette of colours, almost monochromatic in certain instances, to convey the sometimes tragic Biblical images he portrayed, often for ecclesiastical commissions.

He executed many memorial sculptures, centrepieces and such trophies as the one for the Scouts, designed by Sir Robert (later Lord) Baden-Powell and commissioned by Earl Grey, the Governor General of Canada. He nearly always designed the frames for his enamel panels, often in silver, and executed a number of complex sculptures in bronze and in silver set with enamelled panels or sections.

The Birmingham School of Art taught cloisonné, champlevé and Limoges enamelling under Louis Joseph, a Swiss, and Sidney Meteyard. Meteyard (1868-1947) was a fine painter of highly detailed, idealised subjects, strongly influenced by Burne-Jones and late Pre-Raphaelite work, with a very English yearning for the medieval, which he communicated to

above left:
Alexander Fisher, Christ in a Landscape, *enamel and silver portable ikon, presented to Madeleine Wyndham by Arthur Balfour, 29 June, 1897*

above right:
Alexander Fisher, Bhanavar the Beautiful, *enamelled panel in embossed gold patinated frame, inspired by a short story from* The Shaving of Shagpat *by George Moore*

right:
Newcastle Guild of Handicrafts (also known as The Handicraft Company), Hexagonal silver and silver-gilt casket set with six enamel plaques illustrating Chaucer's Man of Law Tale, with chased inscription "Joy of this world for time will not abide from day to night it changeth as the tide," with, an enamelled finial of a seated woman

above:
Alexander Fisher, *Bronze and enamel jewel casket*

right:
Alexander Fisher, *The Bridge of Life, silver and enamel triptych*

his pupils. He exhibited at the Royal Academy in London, the Royal Birmingham Society of Artists and the Paris Salon. Among his pupils were Alfred R. Pearce, Thomas Cuthbertson and Norman Wilkinson, but the most prolific and spectacular former pupil to become an enamel painter was Kate Eadie, who married Meteyard. She won the National Prize in 1912, and later executed jewellery. Her enamels are invariably clear, detailed, rich in colour, and full of literary allusions.

Just as colourful are the enamel paintings of Sir Hubert Herkomer, for which he often devised complex settings. The pair of enamels of Day and Evening are set in matching wrought gilt metal frames, signed with his initials and dated 1898. For other enamel paintings he devised an elaborate shield into which they could be inserted. Born in Germany but living most of his life in England, he expressed his loyalty to the country of his birth by painting an enamel picture of the Kaiser.

Henry Holiday invented a method of giving shape to his enamels by dividing the picture into a number of small curved sections each of which was individually enamelled, after which the various sections were assembled like a leaded window. He managed to execute more than one version of some of his designs. *The Birth of Aphrodite* illustrated here was one he kept for himself, and for which he designed and made the mosaic frame.

In addition to enamel pictures, small enamel panels were made for insertion on the covers of cigarette boxes made by Liberty and by the Guild of Handicrafts; smaller ones were made for belt buckles, brooches, rings, ecclesiastical furnishings and a variety of objets d'art, particularly commemorative or presentation boxes.

Several of the founders of the Arts and Crafts Movement used enamel, particularly on jewellery. One of the most prolific was Nelson Dawson (1859-1942), who studied metalwork and enamelling with Alexander Fisher. He founded the Artificer's Guild in 1901 with one of his employees, Edward Spencer. He had married Edith

Robinson in 1895, and taught her enamelling, after which she was responsible for most of the enamel work they produced.

Phoebe Anna Traquair (1852-1936) was born in Dublin, but moved to Edinburgh after marrying a Scots palaeontologist, Ramsay Traquair, in 1874. She spent several years embroidering, illustrating books, designing bookbindings and decorating churches before studying enamelling with Lady Gibson Carmichael in 1901. From then on she executed a large number of enamelled plaques and panels, many for various churches, as well as pendants and other items of jewellery.

above left:
Kate Eadie, There is Sweet
Music Here That Softer Falls
Than Petals...Music That
Gentler on the Spirit Lies
Than Tired Eyelids Upon
Tired Eyes, *enamelled panel*
in brass and ebonised frame

above right:
Kate Eadie, Saint Cecilia,
enamelled panel

above far right:
Henry Holiday, The Birth of
Aphrodite, *sectional enamel,*
each section curved in bas
relief, in its original glass
mosaic frame

right:
Kate Eadie, The Return of
Excalibur, *enamelled panel*
surrounded by eight further
enamelled sections, relating
the return of King Arthur's
sword to the Lady of the Lake
after his death, c.1903

above:
Phoebe Traquair, Four
enamelled pendants of
religious subjects

right:
Sidney Meteyard, Eurydice,
circular enamelled panel He
also painted the identical
subject against a fuller
background

*Phoebe Traquair, Saint
George, silver and enamel
tryptich*

Phoebe Traquair, Saint Patrick, silver and enamel tryptich

THE NEW SCULPTURE

opposite:
Sir Alfred Gilbert, Perseus
Arming, *bronze*

right:
Walter Rowlands Ingram,
Ariel: On the bat's back I do
fly, *bronze*

Victorian sculpture aspired to massiveness – life-sized or even larger; classicism, in both subject and treatment; and with distinct preference for marble over bronze. This was largely because sculpture was destined for the public place, the museum or the very grand mansion. The almost heretical concept of Hellenic sculpture, which was the perfection against which all later sculpture was to be compared, preferably unfavourably, as polychromatic surfaced timidly, though triumphantly, in John Gibson's *Tinted Venus* in 1862 (although since Gibson executed several versions of this, one should perhaps refer to his "Tinted Venuses"). Colour was appearing more prominently in Continental multi-media sculpture in funereal white marble was replaced in parts or wholly by coloured marbles, lapis lazuli, rock crystal, ivory, and hard, semi-precious stone, often in conjuction with multi-patinated bronze, silver, gold or other metals.

The rise of a new, moneyed middle class brought about a new interest in the creation of small-scale sculpture for domestic use. This need was satisfied for some time by the mass production of copies of classical models. The introduction of the machine invented by Achille Collas in France, patented in 1834, for producing mechanical reductions of large sculpture had brought out the possibility of owning a domestic sized version of an admired sculpture. Bronze casting in Britain was still in a fairly primitive state, using the sand-cast method which was considered adequate for large sculptures. Small scale bronzes, generally placed at the eye level, demanded a much greater amount of hand chasing and finishing from highly experienced workmen, who were not available. The 1870 Franco-Prussian war and the siege of Paris, followed by the ruthless suppression of the Commune by the French army, caused the arrival of many refugees from France to England. Among them were skilled artisans in ceramics, glass and foundry-work. Several new foundries opened for business from the 1890s onward, though

BIOGRAPHIES

Ashbee, Charles Robert (1863-1942)
Articled to G.F. Bodley from 1883 to 1885, he was trained as an architect. Strongly influenced by the ideas of William Morris, he lived in Toynbee Hall in the East End of London and taught evening classes there. As a reaction to the working conditions, he started a school in 1887 and, a year later, the Guild of Handicraft, a craft cooperative based on a medieval guild. The Guild members shared a commitment to high standards of workmanship and improving the quality of life of the workers. Lectures at the school for uneducated working men were given by Guild members and invited artists, designers and specialist craftsmen. The Guild and School moved in 1890 from Toynbee Hall to Essex House in the Mile End Road, producing metal-work, jewellery, furniture and painting, mostly designed by Ashbee, and they exhibited at the Arts and Crafts Exhibitions, at the Vienna Secession, in Paris, Munich and Düsseldorf, and had retail outlets in London. Many of his designs for jewellery, including belt buckles, were based on stylised variations on the pea-cock. In 1898 he set up the Essex House Press there with a printing press, and designed a type-face for it in 1900. He lectured widely and wrote extensively, establishing himself as a campaigning reformer; in an attempt to create a rural haven far from the urban decay and pover-ty of London he moved the Guild to Chipping Campden, Gloucestershire, in 1902. The move soon proved a financial failure, and the Guild went into liquidation in 1908, though several of its craftsmen continued to work independently. Ashbee then returned to architectural practice.

Baillie Scott, Mackay Hugh (1865-1945)
Born in Kent, eldest of fourteen children of a wealthy Scottish Laird with a sheep-farm in Australia, he attended the Royal Agricultural College in Cirencester, but chose instead to become an architect, and was articled to the City Architect of Bath. In 1889 he married and moved to the Isle of Man, setting up as an architect. He met Archibald Knox there and they designed a number of fireplaces and stained glass together. In 1897 he was commissioned to redecorate and furnish the drawing-room and dining-room of the Grand Duke of Hesse in his palace in Darmstadt: the furniture, light fittings and metalwork were designed in collaboration with Ashbee and executed at the Guild of Handicraft's workshops. In 1901 he entered the 'House for an Art Lover' competition organised by the *Zeitschrift für Innendekoration*, for which he received the highest prize actually awarded (the top prize being withheld). He moved to Bedford, and continued to design inlaid and painted furniture for John White's works in Pyghtle, which he had begun to do in 1898, and which was sold through Liberty & Co and

a Bond Street showroom, both in London. He moved several times, and went on designing dwellings and their contents until the outbreak of war in 1939.

Baker, Oliver (1856-1936) Born in Birmingham, the son of a landscape painter and etcher, he studied art under his father and at the Birmingham School of Art, soon establishing himself as a painter and etcher of landscapes and architectural subjects, exhibiting at the Royal Academy, the Royal Institute of Painters in Water-colours and several commercial galleries. In 1898 William Rabone Haseler (1860-1936), a Birmingham manufacturer of jewellery and silver, whose sister was married to Baker's brother, suggested to him the possibility of designing 'an artistic line of silverware.' Baker liked the idea and began drawing but, realising his lack of practical knowledge of the techniques involved, enrolled at the School of Art at the age of 41. He soon produced a wide variety of designs, which Haseler took to London. Liberty's assistant John Llewellyn liked them, showed them to Liberty, and a joint company was formed by Liberty and Haseler, which was to manufacture most of Liberty's silver and pewter designs using the Trade Names of Cymric and Tudric.

Bates, Harry (1850/1-1899) Born in Stevenage, Herts, he worked as an architect's clerk before apprenticeship as a stone carver, modelling class under Jules Dalou, then admission to the Royal Academy Schools in 1881 where he won a Gold Medal and a travelling studentship. He spent two years working in Paris, where he met Rodin. On his return to Britain he executed much architectural decoration in terracotta and stone, several public monuments, and a number of sensitive smaller works in a variety of materials, including *Pandora* in marble, ivory and bronze; and *Mors Janua Vitae* in bronze, ivory and mother-of-pearl. He was a member of the Art Workers' Guild from 1886 and was elected Associate of the Royal Academy in 1892.

Bayes, Gilbert (1872-1953) Born in London, he studied at the City and Guilds School in Finsbury then entered the Royal

Academy Schools in 1896, sponsored by George Frampton. He won a Gold Medal and a travelling studentship which took him to France and Italy. He executed a series of powerful sculptures of knights on horseback, several with a touch of enamel, and female nudes in bronze, including the idealised figure of the *Greek Dancer* and *Reverie*. He executed a number of applied art objects, including caskets, trophy cups, a clock-case, a smoker's cabinet, door fittings, furniture panels, mirrors, stained-glass, medals and medallions; did portrait sculpture, War Memorials, public statuary, garden sculpture including fountains, architectural sculpture and a variety of polychrome designs using coloured stoneware by Royal Doulton. The most spectacular of these is the monumental clock over the main entrance of the Selfridges department store in Oxford Street, the 11ft (3.35 metres) tall figure of *The Queen of Time*. He was a member of the Art Workers' Guild from 1896, becoming its Master in 1925.

Benson, William Arthur Smith (1854-1924) Articled to the architect Basil Champneys, with whom he worked from 1878 to 1880, he met Burne-Jones who introduced him to William Morris. Morris encouraged him to design and manufacture domestic metalwork. He began with a small workshop in 1880, then built a factory in Hammersmith and opened a shop in Bond Street, with a façade designed by him, in 1887. Using a variety of machinery, W.A.S. Benson & Co produced a wide range of copper and brass tableware and lighting which was regularly shown at the Arts and Crafts Exhibitions. He also designed furniture and wallpaper for Morris & Co and furniture for J.S. Henry. On the death of Morris he became a director of the firm. He ceased production and retired in 1920.

BRETBY ART POTTERY Established in Woodville, Burton-on-Trent, about 1882 by Henry Tooth, who had left the Linthorpe Art Pottery, and William Ault. The production consisted of simply designed decorative ceramics in various coloured glazes, its main selling point being its relative cheapness. Ault left the company five years later to set up his

own pottery, eventually using designs by Christopher Dresser. Tooth remained, helped by his son, who took over the running of the pottery in 1914, and his daughters, including Florence who had some talent for design and eventually headed the modelling shop. The firm soon introduced a wide variety of items, including 'Ligna Ware', designed to look like wood bark, 'Copperette Ware', designed to look like hammered copper, 'Clanta Ware', designed to look like ironware, and 'Jewelled Ware', which looked as if it was inlaid with coloured stones. In the late nineties and the early Twentieth Century several items of Art Nouveau design were produced, including tobacco jars with lids incorporating a nymph's head in relief, pots and jardinieres made to look like wood banded with metal hoops, often with coloured 'jewels' and trays and chargers in contrasting colours in abstract patterns in the style of van de Velde.

Brock, Thomas (1847-1922) Born in Worcester, he attended the Government School of Design there, became an assistant of the sculptor J.H. Foley in 1866 and entered the Royal Academy Schools a year later, winning a gold medal in 1869. On Foley's death in 1874 he completed many of his unfinished works and was soon acknowledged. He executed many portrait sculptures and public statuary, the most prominent of the latter being the huge Queen Victoria Memorial opposite Buckingham Palace facing The Mall. His finest figure was the full-length *Eve* (1898), executed in versions in marble and in bronze, in two sizes, each with small but significant changes from each other. He was elected Associate Member of the Royal Academy in 1883, Full Member in 1891, and was a founder member of the Royal Society of British Sculptors. He was knighted in 1911.

Browning, Robert Barrett (1846-1912) Son of the poets Robert and Elizabeth Browning, he studied in Antwerp, Belgium, and in Paris. He exhibited his paintings and sculpture at the Royal Academy from 1878, at the Grafton Gallery and at the Grosvenor Gallery. He exhibited at the International Exhibition in Paris in 1889, and was awarded a Bronze Medal. The bronze statue of *Dryope Fascinated*

by Apollo in the Form of a Serpent was cast in two sizes, the life size one designed for Brighton. The figure stood in his living room, and was the central subject of several of his paintings.

Burne-Jones, Edward Coley (1833-1898) As an undergraduate at Exeter College, Oxford, which he had entered in 1853, he met William Morris, and both decided not to pursue their studies for the Church and take up painting. In 1857 he designed stained glass panels for James Powell and Son and, in 1861, was a founder member of Morris, Marshall, Faulkner and Co. along with Morris, Rossetti, Ford Madox Brown and others. He designed stained glass, tiles and tapestries for the firm and later illustrated books for Morris's Kelmscott Press. He was a very successful painter in oils and watercolours, was elected Associate of the Royal Academy in 1885 and created a baronet in 1894.

Burns, Robert (1869-1941) Born and educated in Edinburgh, he painted in oils and watercolours, was a fine imaginative draughtsman, designer and decorator. He was a regular illustrator for *The Evergreen*, a magazine which also published illustrators and writers from Dundee. Calling himself a 'limner', he executed a number of monochromatic drawings of medieval subjects very much in the English Art Nouveau illustrative style. He was elected an

Associate of the Royal Scottish Academy in 1902 but resigned in 1920.

Butterfield, Lindsay P. He was a prolific designer of wallpapers and textiles, some of which were supplied to Morris & Co, and these were mostly executed by Thomas Wardle & Co of Leek. He also wrote on the theory of design. Many of his designs were based on stylised floral patterns in an Art Nouveau manner.

CHILD & CHILD Firm of jewellers and silversmiths established in London in 1880 by Walter Child and Harold Child. They registered their silver makers' marks at Goldsmiths' Hall, but also used a Trade Mark of CC with a sunflower between on their jewellery cases as well as on the jewels. They executed some pieces of jewellery designed by Burne-Jones, and specialised in finely enamelled brooches, buckles, pendants and larger objects. The firm was given a Royal Warrant for Queen Alexandra. The partnership was dissolved in 1899, but Harold Child continued to trade at the same address until his death in Milan in 1915.

Cooper, John Paul (1869-1933) Born in London, he entered Bradfield College in 1886 where he met Edward Gordon Craig. With no vacancy in Norman Shaw's architectural practice, he entered J.D. Sedding's office in 1889. When

the architect died in 1891, he joined Henry Wilson, who had taken over Sedding's unfinished projects. Architectural work was interspersed with craft work in gesso, in embroidery design, in metal, which he began to exhibit at the Arts and Crafts Society in 1894 and later to sell through Montague Fordham's Gallery in Maddox Street which was to take over the Artificers' Guild in 1903. By 1899 he was almost totally involved in craft work, keeping detailed Stock Books of every completed piece. In 1901 he was appointed Head of the Metalwork Department at the Birmingham School of Art, after taking instructions in jewellery and metalworking from three of Wilson's assistants, John Innocent, Cowell and Latino Movio, while taking a fourth, Lorenzo Colarossi, with him to Birmingham to teach the practical side of silversmithing. He married May Oliver, a second cousin who had been working closely with him. Increasing commissions led to his giving up the Birmingham position in 1907. He produced many items of jewellery, silver and boxes in gesso or shagreen; exhibited at the Decorative Arts of Great Britain and Ireland show at the Louvre in Paris in 1914; and was given a major retrospective at Walker's Galleries in 1931. He joined the Art Workers' Guild in 1908.

Crane, Walter (1845-1915) Trained as a wood engraver, he illustrated many children's books, designed ceramics for Wedgwood from 1867, for Maw & Co from 1874 and lustreware and tiles for the Pilkington Tile and Pottery Co from 1900. He also designed stained glass, wallpapers, and embroidered, woven and printed textiles, as well as banners and political pamphlets for the Socialist League. He wrote several influential books on design theory and designed and illustrated many volumes of poetry and other works. He painted a number of large compositions of Symbolist inspiration, and greatly influenced Continental Art Nouveau artists such as Henry van de Velde, though he ostensibly rejected them. He was a founder member of the Art Workers' Guild and the Arts and Crafts Exhibition Society of which he was President from 1887 to 1912 except for the 1893 to 1896 years when he was Director of Design at the Manchester School of Art.

Cuzner, Bernard (1877-1956) A student at the Vittoria Street School from 1896, then at the Margaret Street School from 1899, he later taught at both Schools, remaining at Margaret Street from 1911 to 1942. He designed both jewellery and silver in an Art Nouveau aesthetic, though he later moved away from it. Much of the jewellery was inspired by the work of the Gaskins, though the range of his enamelling included niello inlay. Unlike so many other Arts and Crafts designers, he had no qualms about using machinery to simplify work. He supplied Liberty & Co with a number of designs through the Haseler firm, by which he was employed for several years, and wrote a Silver-smithing Manual which was published in 1935.

Dawson, Nelson (1859-1942) Born in Lincolnshire, he trained as an architect, then studied painting at the South Kensington Schools. His interest in metalwork began in 1881, and he studied enamelling with Alexander Fisher. In 1893 he married Edith Brearey Robinson (1862-1920), a Scarborough girl from a Quaker family, and taught her enamelling; they were to execute a large quantity of enamelled jewellery, buckles, boxes and other objects, employing several assistants. In association with his wife and Edward Spencer (1872-1938), one of his assistants, he

founded the Artificers' Guild in 1901 in his Chiswick workshop, but it was taken over by Montague Fordham, former director of the Birmingham Guild of Handicraft, in 1903 and transferred to Maddox Street, where Spencer became Chief Designer, though John Paul Cooper supplied the Guild with many designs. The Guild failed in 1905 because of under-capitalisation. Spencer set up the Guild of St. Michael, but it did not last, and he then recreated the Artificers' Guild in 1907 in his complete control with premises in Conduit Street and designs by Henry Wilson, May Morris (William's daughter), Phoebe Traquair, John Paul Cooper, and others. The Guild survived Spencer's death until 1942. Nelson Dawson gave up metalworking in 1914 to concentrate on painting and etching, executing many marine subjects and landscapes of Yorkshire, East Anglia and the east coast, exhibiting at the Royal Water-colour Society, to which he was elected associate in 1921, the Royal Society of British Artists, the Royal Society of Painter-Etchers and Engravers, to which he was elected Member in 1915, the Royal West of England Academy and the International Society of Sculptors, Painters and Gravers. Edith Dawson exhibited flower paintings.

De Morgan, William Frend (1839-1917) Born in London, he studied at the Royal Academy Schools and was introduced to William Morris and Burne-Jones by fellow-student, Henry Holiday, and through them to Rossetti and the other Pre-Raphaelites. He began designing tiles and stained glass for Morris's new company, but unhappy about the way his designs were executed, set up a kiln in the basement of his house, experimenting with lustre decoration on the tiles. In 1871 he moved to Cheyne Row, where he was assisted by the brothers Charles and Fred Passenger, who were to stay with him for some thirty years, and later also by Joe Juster. In 1881 he moved to Merton Abbey, closer to Morris's new workshops, but his uncertain health caused him to move in 1888 to Sands End, Fulham, where he went into partnership with the architect Halsey Ricardo. The partnership ended in 1898 but he remained active in the business until 1905, after which he turned to writing a series of successful novels. He spent

considerable time in Florence from 1892 and some of his designs were produced by the Italian ceramics firm of Cantigalli. In 1885 he had married the painter Evelyn Pickering (1855-1919), who had studied with her uncle, R. Spencer Stanhope and at the Slade School. Her Idealist, Symbolist pictures influenced her husband in his choice of some subjects for his pots. She exhibited at the Grosvenor and New Galleries in London.

DELLA ROBBIA Co. Ltd. Set up at Birkenhead, a town on the banks of the River Mersey opposite Liverpool in 1894 by Conrad Dressler and Harold Rathbone (1858-1920), a painter who had studied with Ford Madox Brown, and was a cousin of R. Llewellyn Rathbone. It was formed under the supervision of a controlling council which included Harold Rathbone's father Philip Henry Rathbone and the painters G.F. Watts and William Holman Hunt. Intended primarily to produce decorative architectural elements, the firm also produced tiles and hollow-wares, often decorated in sgraffito. Most of the modellers and decorators were recruited from local art schools, though Carlo Manzoni joined them in 1897 from the Granville Pottery in Hanley, and some low relief plaques were made to designs by Robert Anning Bell, then head of the Liverpool School of Architecture. He also designed the galleon device which was used as a Trade Mark on many of the pottery's works. Other designers for the firm included Conrad Dressler, Cassandia Ann Walker and Marianne de Caluwé and her husband, while designs were executed after Burne-Jones and Ford Madox Brown. The firm closed down in 1906.

Dressler, Conrad (1856-1940) Born in London of German parentage, he studied modelling under Lanteri at the National Art Training School in South Kensington, travelled in France, and was befriended by Ruskin. In 1894 he moved to Birkenhead and joined Harold Rathbone at the Della Robbia Pottery. Three years later he joined the Medmenham Pottery at Marlow. He designed there a 150 foot faience frieze for the Lever Bros. Factory in Port Sunlight. He executed portrait busts, decorative figurative sculpture for Colleges,

Churches and other architectural sites, and later lived in the United States and France. He joined the Art Workers' Guild in 1891.

Drury, Alfred (1856-1944) Born in London, he studied at the Oxford School of Art then at the South Kensington Schools where he studied modelling with Jules Dalou then with Edward Lanteri, and won gold medals in the National Art Competitions in 1879, 1880 and 1881. He joined Dalou in Paris as his assistant from 1881 to 1885, taught at the Wimbledon School of Art between 1892 and 1893, and executed a large number of architectural, memorial and decorative statues for Vauxhall Bridge, the War Office, the façade of the Victoria and Albert Museum in London as well as venues in Leeds, Bradford and Bristol. He executed several smaller scale sculptures, including *Circe* and *The Age of Innocence*, both of which were exhibited at the International Exhibition in Paris in 1900, for which he was awarded a Gold Medal. He joined the Art Workers' Guild in 1899 and was elected a Full Member of the Royal Academy in 1913.

Eadie, Kate M. (1878-1945) Studied at the Birmingham School of Art, and became one of the most talented enamel artists. She began to produce pictorial enamels from 1904, frequently based on medieval romance, the Arthurian cycle and romantic imagery inspired by Burne-Jones.

She was a member of the Royal Society of Miniature Painters and an Associate of the Royal Birmingham Society of Artists, exhibiting in both as well as in the Paris Salon. In addition to enamels and painted miniatures she designed jewellery in the Arts and Crafts style. She married Sidney Meteyard.

Fisher, Alexander (1864-1936) Son of a potter who enamelled on ceramics, he studied at the South Kensington Schools from 1884 to 1886, and a series of lectures and demonstrations on enamelling by Louis Dalpayrat of the Sèvres Manufactory fired his determination to study the techniques involved. A travelling scholarship enabled him to study in France and Italy, and he set up a workshop on his return to England. He became head tutor for teaching enamelling techniques at the Central School of Art from 1896 to 1899; he went into partnership with Henry Wilson, also at the Central School, but their temperaments were too different and they broke up. He exhibited at the Arts and Crafts Exhibition Society and wrote extensively on the technique, encouraging both professional jewellers and gifted amateurs to seek his instruction. His professional pupils included Nelson Dawson, Ernestine Mills, the Gaskins, Sidney Meteyard and Kate Eadie; amateurs included those leading members of the group known as 'The Souls', the Honourable Mrs. Percy Wyndham, in whose

home in Belgrave Square he exhibited several pieces, and her daughter, Lady Elcho. Even enamellers such as Phoebe Traquair or Edith Dawson who did not directly follow his instruction were technically and stylistically influenced by him. In 1904 he set up his own school of enamelling in his Warwick Gardens studio.

Fitchew, Dorothy Daughter of an artist and steel engraver, she produced many illustrations for *The Harmsworth Magazine* and other publications in the 1890s and designed fabrics and wallpapers in floral Art Nouveau patterns. She executed many watercolours in a Fairy-Symbolist style influenced by Rossetti and Burne-Jones.

Ford, Edward Onslow (1852-1901) Born in London, he studied painting at the Antwerp Academy in Belgium in 1870 and in Munich, Germany from 1871 to 1872 where he developed an interest in sculpture. After his return to London, his admiration for Alfred Gilbert led him to execute several idealised nudes and busts which Susan Beattie has described as "imbued with delicate, melancholy, symbolism." He exhibited at the Royal Academy from 1875, and was elected to it in 1895. He showed five works at the Paris International Exhibition in 1900, in which he was also a Member of the Jury. He executed a number of public monuments and, in addition to his sculptures in bronze or marble, essayed a multimedia figure of St. George and the Dragon in silver, ivory and marble. He was a member of the Art Workers' Guild from 1884, becoming its Master in 1895.

Frampton, George James (1860-1928)
Born in London, he worked in an architect's office before becoming apprenticed to a firm of architectural stone carvers. In 1880 he joined W.S. Frith's modelling class at the South London Technical Art School in Lambeth, then entered the Royal Academy Schools in 1881, winning a Gold Medal and a travelling studentship in 1887 which enabled him to go to Paris as a pupil of Antonin Mercié. Returning to London in 1889, he taught sculpture at the Slade School, was appointed joint head of the Central School of Art and Crafts with W.R. Lethaby, wrote for *The Studio* magazine, exhibited at the *Libre Esthétique* in Brussels and the Vienna Secession in 1898 and the International Exhibition in Paris in 1900 in which he was awarded a Grand Prix. He designed jewellery, medals, household fittings which he frequently exhibited at the Arts and Crafts Exhibition Society; portrait busts, architectural sculpture, monuments and memorials as well as relief decoration, including the ever-youthful figure of *Peter Pan* in Kensington Gardens. He executed only a few strange aetherial Symbolist busts, the most successful being the *Mysteriarch*, a polychrome plaster of 1893 and *Lamia* in 1900, which exists in two versions, a painted plaster one and another of bronze and ivory set with opals. He joined the Art Workers' Guild in 1887, becoming Master in 1902, was elected Full Member of the Royal Academy in 1902, was a founder member of the Royal Society of British Sculptors, and was knighted in 1908.

Gaskin, Arthur Joseph (1862-1928) Born in Birmingham, he studied at the School of Art there where he was taught tempera painting by Joseph Southall. He illustrated a number of books, including *Shepherd's Callendar* which was printed and published by William Morris at his Kelmscott Press in 1897, and tales by Hans Christian Andersen (1893) and the Brothers Grimm (1899). He taught part-time at the School of Art and succeeded R. Catterson-Smith as Headmaster of the Vittoria Street School in 1902. He exhibited paintings and etchings, mostly portraits, figures and still life subjects, at the Royal Birmingham Society of Artists between 1883 and 1928 and was elected an Associate Member of it in 1903 and a Full Member in 1927. He exhibited at the main London Galleries from 1891 and was a member of the Art Workers' Guild. He lived in Warwickshire for several years then retired to Chipping Campden, Gloucestershire, where C.R. Ashbee's Guild of Handicraft had moved; he died there. He married Georgina Cave France (1868-1934), who had also studied at the School of Art in 1894. They began producing jewellery about 1890, Georgina doing the designing and her husband the enamelling, the work being carried out by their assistants or at the works of A.E. Jones. They supplied Liberty & Co with some designs.

Gilbert, Alfred (1854-1934) Born in London, his original intention of becoming a surgeon was thwarted when he failed his entrance examination at the Middlesex Hospital. He entered the Royal Academy Schools in 1873 then, three years later, went to Paris to study at the Ecole des Beaux-Arts after which he spent six years in Italy. He was one of the first to revive lost-wax casting in England, and was commissioned to execute a number of public Memorials, including the Shaftesbury Memorial in Piccadilly Circus entitled *The Spirit of Christian Charity*, surmounted by the figure of *Anteros, Agape*, representing selfless love, but ever since familiarly known as *Eros*. It was to bring a storm of shocked anger his way. In 1892 he began to design the tomb of the Duke of Clarence at Windsor, a major commission for the Royal Family which was only completed in 1926. He also worked as a jeweller and silversmith, designing a Mayoral Chain for the city of Preston and a spectacular epergne in silver, bronze, ivory and mother-of-pearl presented to Queen Victoria by the Army on her Jubilee, and currently on view at the Victoria and Albert Museum, as well as cups, a ewer, sets of spoons and other items. In 1900 he was appointed Professor of Sculpture at the Royal Academy, but a year later, harassed by debts and an inability to complete commissions on time, he declared himself bankrupt and went to Bruges for over twenty years, returning in 1926 to complete the Clarence tomb. This was surrounded by polychromed Symbolist statuettes, densely structured figures in great contrast to his other great Symbolist figures, the smooth, simplified, homo-erotic, idealised self portraits such as *Icarus* and *Comedy and Tragedy*. He joined the Art Workers' Guild in 1888 was elected Member of the Royal Academy in 1892, and was knighted in 1932.

Gilmour, Margaret (1860-1942) After studying at the Glasgow School of Art she set up a studio in West George Street, Glasgow in 1893 with her sister Mary Ann Bell Gilmour (1872-1938), while a younger sister, Agnes, kept the accounts. Both sisters were highly accomplished in the crafts, but Margaret was the principal designer, and had a display of her personal beaten brass and copperwork at the Glasgow International Exhibition in 1901. They maintained the studio for the rest of their lives, executing commissions for mirrors, clocks, candlesticks, desk sets, jardinières, toiletry sets or fireplace surrounds in 'The Glasgow Style', their hand-beaten metalwork often highlighted by small enamelled sections. In addition the Gilmour Studio also taught a variety of crafts, including metalwork, leatherwork, embroidery, wood carving, wood staining, ceramic decoration and painting at all levels of competence.

Haité, George Charles (1855-1924) Almost entirely self-taught, he came to London in 1873, and spent several years designing wallpapers, leaded glass and metalwork. As a landscape painter in oils and watercolours he exhibited at the Royal Academy from 1883, was President of the Langham Sketching Club between 1883 and 1887 and again in 1908; President of the London Sketch Club; President of the Institute of Decorative Designers; Member of the Royal Institute of Painters in Water-colours; Member of the Royal Institute of Oil Painters; Member of the Royal Society of British Artists; and Member of the Royal British Colonial Society of Artists. In the late nineties he designed several complex largely monochromatic raised

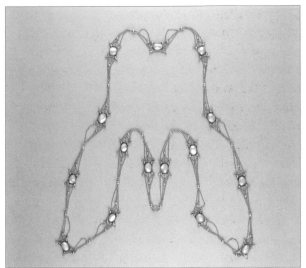 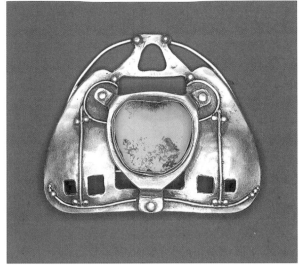

patterns in the Art Nouveau style for the Ana-glypta range of the Wallpaper Manufacture Company of Darwen.

Harris, Kate   Designer of silver for William Hutton & Sons, the firm originally founded in Birmingham in 1800 but transferred to Sheffield two years later. Several members of the Hutton family ran the firm which was turned into a limited liability company in 1893 with premises in Sheffield and London, expanding back to Birmingham in 1899. Kate Harris was praised for her designs in *The Studio* in October 1901. While the firm's chief designer from 1880 to 1914 was Swaffield Brown, Kate Harris designed buckles, toiletry sets and other small silver items in an Art Nouveau style, some pieces with blue/green enamel, others set with mother-of-pearl.

Holiday, Henry (1839-1927)   Born in London, he entered the Royal Academy Schools at the age of fifteen, his fellow pupils including Simeon Solomon, William De Morgan and William Blake Richmond, and was introduced into the Pre-Raphaelite circle. He joined Powells of Whitefriars as principal stained glass designer in succession to Burne-Jones and supplied Morris's company with many designs. He became interested in mosaics, enamelling and sculpture, mastering all three disciplines, and invented a means of producing enamelled

pictures in relief by cutting up the projected image as a leaded glass window, shaping each little section, enamelling each separately then assembling them into a whole. He exhibited his genre and historical paintings at the Royal Academy from 1858, selling his first painting on the first exhibition day. He designed embroideries which were usually executed by his wife Catherine, who also supplied Morris & Co with embroidered panels. He was also a successful mural painter and in 1890 founded his own glassworks.

HORNER, CHARLES   Firm of jewellers established in Halifax, Yorkshire by Charles Horner in the mid 1850s, later inventing the 'Dorcas' thimble. On his death in 1896 two of his six sons, James Dobson Horner and C. Harry Horner became managing partners, built a new factory, and expanded production into small, inexpensive items of jewellery in enamelled pressed silver in the Art Nouveau style popularised by Liberty & Co., while still manufacturing a wide range of thimbles in gold and in silver, and producing a few items designed by Edgar Simpson. In 1909 it became a limited liability company. Most of its gold and silver products were assayed in Chester.

Howarth, Albany E. (1872-1936)   Etcher, lithographer and water-colourist, he worked in England, France and Italy, mostly exhibiting

landscapes and architectural subjects, though his figures are full-blown Art Nouveau, clearly influenced by Mucha and Privat-Livemont. He exhibited at the Royal Academy from 1906 and at the Royal Society of Painter-Etchers and Engravers, to which he was elected Associate in 1910. An exhibition of his work was held at Dowdeswell's Galleries in London in 1912.

Jackson, Frederick Hamilton (1848-1923)   After studying at the Royal Academy Schools, he exhibited landscapes, seascapes and genre paintings and water-colours at the leading London galleries from 1870. He was Master of the Antique School at the Slade under Poynter and Legros and founded the Chiswick School of Art with E.S. Burchett in 1880. He wrote *Handbooks for the Designer and Craftsman* and other works, was a member of the Art Workers' Guild from 1887 and of the Royal Society of British Artists from 1889. He painted a few imaginative Symbolist pictures of idealised imagery.

Jahn, A.C.C.   Headmaster of the Municipal School of Art, Wolverhampton. He designed and made some items of jewellery which incorporate female profiles in a tentative Art Nouveau style.

Jones, Albert Edward (1879-1954)   Born into a Birmingham family of metalworkers, he learned his trade at the firm of John Hardman before joining the Birmingham Guild of Handicraft in about 1900-01. In 1902 he set up his own business with two employees; in 1906 he opened new workshops from which he advertised himself as "Art Silversmith, Maker of Hand-Beaten Silver Wares. Rose Bowls, Challenge Cups, Caskets, Candlesticks, Tea Sets, Tea Caddies, Pepper Castors, Mustard Pots, etc." Although his was very much a commercial enterprise, Jones was a thorough Art & Crafts designer, imbued with the ideals of the Guild of Handicraft, even refusing, for many years, to make electro-plated wares. He exhibited at Arts & Crafts and Jewellers' Exhibitions, occasionally employed Bernard Cuzner, and executed many pieces for the Gaskins and other Vittoria Street School designers. In 1912 he exhibited examples of St. Dunstan's Ware, delicately tinted copper-bronze through patination, mounted in silver, which had originally been developed in Liverpool by Richard Rathbone then brought to the Birmingham firm of The Faulkner Bronze Company by one of Rathbone's workers, F.W. Salthouse; Jones first acquired an interest in the technique in about 1905, eventually taking over both the Trade Mark and the services of Salthouse. Many of A.E. Jones's wares were retailed in London by G.L. Connell of Cheapside.

King, Jessie Marion (1875-1949)   Born in Glasgow, she studied at the Glasgow School of Art where she won a travelling scholarship which took her to Italy and Germany. She taught in the Design School at the Glasgow School of Art and participated in several international exhibitions. She illustrated a large number of books, often choosing romantic medieval subjects, and designed many commercial book covers in Britain and Germany, as well as several sumptuous individual ones in gilt-decorated parchment. In 1908 she married E.A. Taylor and they moved to Salford, then to Paris, returning to Britain as war broke out in 1914. She later worked in batik, writing a book about the technique, and designed murals which were stencilled on the walls of several schools She designed jewellery, buckles and silver for Liberty & Co. In later life she painted blank cups and saucers which she sold in Kirkcudbright, where she lived.

Knox, Archibald (1864-1933)   Born in Cronkbourne on the Isle of Man, he studied at the Douglas (IoM) School of Art, steeping himself in Celtic lore. He taught there until 1888; in 1897 he moved to a school in Redhill, Surrey. He then began designing for a variety of materials at the Silver Studio, through which he began designing for Liberty & Co. Most of the early designs in jewellery, silver and pewter in the Cymric and Tudric ranges were by him, or slight variations of his designs, and he was largely responsible for the course of the Liberty Style and its development as Celtically-inspired Art Nouveau, though it was, of course, also the taste of Liberty himself. He returned to the Isle of Man in 1900, but four years later was teaching at Kingston School of Art, moved to the United States in 1912 but found it difficult to establish himself there and returned to the Isle of Man a year later. He continued to submit designs for carpets, textiles and garden pots to Liberty in addition to silver, pewter and jewellery. His last commission for Arthur Lasenby Liberty was the design for his grave stone.

Lanteri, Edward (1848-1917)   Born in Auxerre, Burgundy, he studied art in Paris at the Ecole des Beaux-Arts. In 1872 he moved to London, joined the staff of the Royal College of Art in 1874 and was appointed Professor of Sculpture from 1880 to 1910. He exhibited at the Royal Academy from 1876, and executed many portrait busts and figures and public statuary. He was a Fellow of the Royal Society of British Sculptors.

Lucchesi, Andrea Carlo (1860-1925)   Born in London, the son of an Italian sculptor, he studied at the West London School of Art, then worked as assistant to several sculptors, including Edward Onslow Ford; he also worked for several commercial silversmiths, and entered the Royal Academy Schools in 1886. He executed several life-sized sculptures as well as reductions, specialising in idealised female figures, often nude, in Symbolist poses, yet with vivid, lively expressions. Two of his life-sized plaster figures exhibited in Paris at the 1900 International Exhibition brought him a Gold Medal. He joined the Art Workers' Guild in 1907.

Mackennal, Bertram (1863-1931)   Born in Melbourne, Australia, of Scottish parents, he studied with his father, an architectural carver, then at the National Gallery Art School. He arrived in London in 1882, entering the Royal Academy Schools a year later, though after only a few months he moved to Paris where he studied with Rodin. In 1886 he was appointed head of the modelling and design department at the Coalport Potteries in Shropshire but returned to Australia two years later and after a few years was back in Paris. He exhibited his first major Symbolist work, *Circe*, at the Paris Salon in 1893 to great acclaim, but when it was shown at the Royal Academy in London the following year the writhing figures on the base were considered too provocatively erotic, and were chastely covered with a sheet. Settling in London, he executed several small sculptures as well as doorplates, handles, switches and doorbells. He executed architectural sculptures, monuments and war memorials, yet always returned to idealised Symbolist figures. He joined the Art Workers' Guild in 1905, was elected Full Member of the Royal Academy in 1922 and was knighted in 1921.

Mackmurdo, Arthur Heygate (1851-1942)   He was apprenticed to T. Chatfield Clarke then became a pupil of James Brooks in 1869. In 1873 he attended Ruskin's lectures as Slade Professor at Oxford and travelled to Italy with him a year later. In 1875 he set up his architectural practice in London. Two years later he met William Morris, who aroused his interest in the applied arts. In 1882 he set up the Century Guild to 'render all branches of art the sphere no longer of the tradesman but of the artist.' The magazine *The Hobby Horse*, published by his friend George Allen first appeared in 1884. One of the earliest examples of Art Nouveau design appeared in his cover design for *Wren's City Churches* and in the fretwork pattern on the back of a chair. As an old man he gave up the practice of architecture and spent his time formulating theories on currency reform.

MARCH BROTHERS   Consisting of at least five brothers and one sister, the March family lived in Farnborough, Kent on an

right:
Arthur Robertson, The tomb of the Duke of Clarence at Windsor, *designed and executed by Alfred Gilbert between 1892 and 1926. Watercolour and gouache done as a presentation of the projected scheme, 1894*

estate called Goddendene which, in addition to their home, housed an extensive workshop, a casting pit, furnaces, a powerful hoist and their own small railway system. March Brothers produced a wide range of metalwork in both Arts & Crafts and Art Nouveau styles, including candlesticks, clocks, door furniture, overmantels, plaques, mirror frames and lanterns, some inlaid with enamels or mother of pearl, usually marked 'M.Bros', as well as several items of silver and gold jewellery. In addition, several of the siblings were fine sculptors. Among them was Sydney March, who executed an equestrian bronze statue of King Edward VIIth and several memorial sculptures, including one of a sad angel commemorating his parents; Edward March (1873-1941); Vernon March (1891-1930), who designed the Champlain monument in Ontario, Canada; and Elsie March, who exhibited at the Royal Academy, the Royal Society of British Artists, to which she was elected member, and the Royal Glasgow Institute of Fine Arts. They all also executed many fine small bronze figures of nudes, naiads, mermaids, fairies and other charmingly mysterious creatures.

Marks, Gilbert (1861-1905)   Took up an apprenticeship with the retail and wholesale firm of Johnson, Walker & Tolhurst, goldsmiths, silversmiths and jewellers, in 1878, shortly after leaving school. He was to spend seven years

there, after which he set up his own workshop. He totally rejected the use of any dies, machinery, or other mechanical aids to production, and insisted on each of his silver productions being designed and made entirely by hand and remaining unique. In 1895 he held his first exhibition of forty items at Johnson, Walker & Tolhurst. It proved highly successful, and he held an annual exhibition there for several years. In 1896 he entered his own mark at Goldsmiths Hall, and often worked with Latino Movio, who had worked for Holland, Aldwinckle & Slater. He died at the age of 44, having produced only about 750 designs in silver, most of which were commissioned. Flowers were his main source of inspiration for decoration, which was often repoussé. He was considered 'one of the most skilful artist-craftsmen' in the country.

Marriott, Ernest (1882-1918)   Born in Manchester, he studied at the Manchester School of Art under Walter Crane. He later became Gordon Craig's Chief Assistant at the School for the Art of the Theatre. He lived and died in Manchester, and painted many European scenes.

Marriott, Frank Pickford (1876-)   Born at Coalbrookdale, Shropshire, he was the brother of Frederick Marriott. Educated in Brisbane, Australia, he returned to England, studied at Goldsmiths College School of Art, then at the

Royal College of Art, obtaining his diploma in 1912. He received national silver and bronze medals, a London County Council Scholarship, a National Scholarship and Senior National Scholarship, after which he exhibited at the Royal Academy in London, the Royal Scottish Academy, various provincial galleries and in the Paris Salon. He painted in tempera, was a mosaic artist, executed several bronzes and worked with stained glass. He was a Member of the Society of Mural Decorators and Painters in Tempera. He later moved to South Africa, where he lived in Port Elizabeth, and became Vice-President of the South African Institute of Art. He collaborated with his brother Frederick on some pictures made of gesso set with mother-of-pearl.

Marriott, Frederick (1860-1941)   Born in Stoke-on-Trent, he was the brother of Frank Pickford Marriott. He studied at the School of Art, Coalbrookdale, then became a pottery painter at Maw & Co at the age of fourteen. He later moved to London, where he studied engraving at the Kensington Museum Schools, gaining a National Art Scholarship to study at the Royal College of Art in 1879. Three years later he went to work for Marcus Ward and Company as designer and illustrator, then was appointed Chief Designer for Eyre and Spottiswood, remaining there for four and a half years. He executed repoussé work, enamelling, wood carving, bookbindings, lithographs, etchings, mezzotints, painting on gesso and modelling, and devised panels in modelled glass with mother-of-pearl inlay. He executed many multi-media pictures on gesso inlaid with mother-of-pearl, using a variety of delicately coloured shells, whose range of colours was extended by boiling the shells with appropriate dyes then polishing them with emery and putty powders, then with rouge and oil; he worked on a few of these with his brother. The panels were then covered in gold leaf or platinum leaf and painted over, sometimes set with gemstones. A full description of his technique in his own words is quoted in an article by Philippe Garner in *Bulletin Number 1* of the Decorative Arts Society. These pictures included such Symbolist titles as *The Angel of Night*, the chivalrous subject of a knight in armour in a tournament, and portraits of Titania and Oberon, Queen and King of the Fairies. He exhibited at the Royal Academy from 1891, the Royal Society of Painter-Etchers and Engravers and the Royal Institute of Oil Painters, in provincial galleries and the Paris Salon. He became Design Master at Blackheath Art School, Headmaster of the Onslow College Art School in Chelsea and Headmaster of Goldsmiths Institute from 1895 to 1925. He was a Member of the Arts and Crafts Society and of the Art Workers' Guild, and was elected an Associate of The Royal Society of Painter-Etchers and Engravers in 1909 and a Full Member in 1924. He painted many architectural scenes in Europe and went on a painting visit to Australia in 1910. He was also elected a Member of the Royal British Colonial Society of Artists, and an Associate of the Royal College of Art.

Meteyard, Sidney Harold (1868-1947) Studied at the Birmingham School of Art under Edward R. Taylor, then taught enamelling at Margaret Street. As a painter of portraits and figure subjects, he often produced pictorial enamels similar and occasionally identical to some of his paintings, though not, of course, in size. He exhibited at the Royal Academy, the Paris Salon and the Royal Birmingham Society of Artists, to which he was elected an Associate in 1902 and Full Member in 1908. He married the artist Kate M. Eadie.

Mills, Ernestine (1871-1959) Born Ernestine Bell, she studied at the Slade School and the Royal College of Art under Alexander Fisher. She was a metal-worker, enameller and painter and executed a large number of War Memorials for churches, hospitals and institutions. She was a member of the Society of Women Artists and was active in the campaigns for Women's Suffrage.

MINTONS Established in 1793 by Thomas Minton. In 1871 the firm set up an Art Pottery in South Kensington under the direction of William Stephen Coleman (1829-1904), a painter in oils and water-colours who specialised in depicting children and young girls at rest and play. He illustrated several children's books, and decorated tiles and plates with similar subjects: Lewis Carroll had a collection of his works. Coleman left in 1873 and the Studio burnt down two years later. The Art Pottery had been open to young artists, many of whom contributed designs for tiles, but most Minton tiles were marketed through a subsidiary company, Minton, Hollis & Co. Some of the most interesting Studio tiles were designed by Walter Crane and E.J. Poynter, who decorated the tile panels in the grill-room of the South Kensington Museum, now the Victoria and Albert Museum. Leon. V. Solon, son of the man who had developed the pâte-sur-pâte technique at Sèvres, took over as Art Director in 1901 and, with John William Wadsworth, introduced a new line called Secessionist Ware. This consisted of simplified Art Nouveau decoration applied to a wide range of goods, including candlesticks, vases, jardinieres and pedestals and tea sets in rich, contrasting colours, such as red and green or red and yellow. Solon left in 1909, and was succeeded by Wadsworth, who introduced Art Nouveau floral patterns. Solon, who had decorated a number of plaques and vases for Minton, later produced many tiles and vases with charming Fairyland and Arabian Nights designs under his own name.

Moira, Gerald (1867-1959) Born in London of Portuguese parents, he studied at the Royal Academy Schools and in Paris. He exhibited at the Royal Academy from 1891 and the International Society from 1899 and

was a founder Member of the National Portrait Society in 1911. He was Professor at the Royal College of Art from 1900 to 1922, then Principal of Edinburgh College of Art from 1924 to 1932. He was elected Associate of the Royal Society of Painters in Water-colours in 1917, Full Member in 1932, and Vice-President in 1953; Member of the Royal West of England Academy in 1919; and President of the Royal Institute of Oil Painters in 1945. He painted several important mural decorations, including the Central Criminal Court, Lloyd's Register and the Wigmore Hall, all in London.

Naper, Ella (1886-1972) Born Ella Louise Champion in New Cross, London, she studied at the Camberwell School of Arts and Crafts from 1904 to 1906 with Fred Partridge before moving to Branscombe in Devon where she spent three years working with him making jewellery and enamels. In 1910 she married Charles Naper, a landscape painter who exhibited at the Royal Academy from 1910 to 1933 but sold very little, and they moved first to Looe in Cornwall, then in 1912 to the artists' colony at Lamorna. She continued making jewellery, often to private commissions, and some of which she may have supplied to Liberty, and exhibited at the Arts and Crafts Exhibition Society and the Women's Art Exhibition in 1931. She executed a number of memorials in pewter and enamel, generally sited in churches. After the First World War she set up and ran the Lamorna Pottery, exhibiting some of her stoneware at the Arts and Crafts Exhibition at Burlington House in London in 1926 alongside the work of Bernard Leach and Shoji Hamada. She developed a close friendship with Laura Knight, whom she taught the art of enamelling, and often posed for her - the beautiful nude model in the spectacular self-portrait of Laura Knight painting, now at the National Portrait Gallery, is Ella Naper.

Neatby, William James (1860-1910) Born in Barnsley, he was a painter in oils and water-colours, architect, muralist and decorator. As head of the architectural department at the Royal Doulton firm from 1890 to 1907, he frequently used Carraraware, a matt stoneware with a crystalline glaze, developed in 1888 and resembling Carrara marble. Coated with enamel while still unfired, then subjected to a single high firing, the resulting glaze was both strong and impervious to atmosphere and was available in a wide range of colours. Neatby designed the façade of the Everard Building in Broad Street, Bristol, in 1901, turning it into a polychrome ceramic mural on the history of printing, with images of Gutenberg and William Morris on either side of the Spirit of Literature, another figure being the Spirit of Truth and Light. When first shown, the façade caused traffic jams for a week as people drove by to see the spectacle. He modelled friezes, caryatids and masks in Carraraware and terracotta, developed Pareanware, earthenware with an eggshell matt finish, and Polychrome Stoneware, an impermeable material with the look of majolica. He designed many tile panels for interiors and exteriors in an Art Nouveau style, including the tile panels in the Meat Hall in Harrods Department Store. His watercolours, some on parchment, are often embellished with touches of gold and silver.

Partridge, Frederick James (1877-1942)
Son of a Barnstaple chemist, he studied at the Birmingham Municipal School of Art from 1899 to 1901, after which he attended a class in Barnstaple run by Jack Baily, a silversmith from the Guild of Handicraft. He joined Ashbee's Guild of Handicraft a year later at Chipping Campden, exhibiting with it at the Arts and Crafts Exhibition Society in 1903, but was dismissed the following year by Ashbee for flirting with a female member of the Guild. He soon opened a workshop in Soho in London, designing and executing delicate jewellery made of horn and enamelled gold and silver, some of which he sold to Liberty & Co. He also worked in Branscombe, Devon, between 1900 and 1908, during which time he worked with, and taught Ella Naper. He married May Hart in 1906. She, too, was a fine enameller, and did some work for Ashbee's Guild of Handicraft.

Pegram, Henry Alfred (1862-1937)   Born in London, he studied at the West London School of Art then entered the Royal Academy Schools in 1881. He won minor prizes in the National Competitions in 1881 and 1883 and prizes at

the School in 1882, 1884 and 1886 after which he worked as an assistant to Hamo Thornycroft from 1887 to 1891. He later executed considerable architectural decorative work as well as some smaller scale Symbolist subjects. He joined the Art Workers' Guild in 1890 and was elected Full Member to the Royal Academy in 1922.

Ramsden, Omar (1873-1939) and **Alwyn Carr** (1872-1940)   They met while both were students at the Sheffield School of Art. In 1898 they set up in business together beginning by executing a mace for the City of Sheffield, a competition-winner designed by Ramsden. Together they designed and executed a variety of silver and jewellery, some of it with enamel, much of it of Art Nouveau inspiration. Many of their designs were religiously inspired by their common Roman Catholic backgrounds and beliefs, and Ramsden became chairman of the Church Crafts League. They employed several workers, and often used machinery on multiple pieces. Carr served in the First World War and returned injured. Their attempt to resume the business partnership failed, and it was dissolved in 1919, after which each worked independently.

Rathbone, Richard Llewellyn Benson (1864-1939)   The Rathbones were a family of Unitarian merchants in Liverpool, several of whose members were in the forefront of progressive taste there in the 1880s and 1890s. Edmund Rathbone was the Century Guild's representative in Liverpool; Harold Rathbone, who had studied under Ford Madox Brown, ran the Della Robbia Pottery in Birkenhead, Philip Rathbone was a Chairman of the Fine Arts Committee; Richard taught metalwork in the Applied Art Section of Liverpool University's School of Architecture, set up in 1894, in which Robert Anning Bell also worked. They were joined by Herbert McNair who with his wife Frances Macdonald designed a few items of jewellery, a tea caddy and caddy spoon and probably a few more items, all of which were executed by Richard Rathbone. In 1905 the Applied Art Section was hived off the University and annexed to the new Municipal School of Art. McNair lost his job. Richard Rathbone, who had set up an active Arts and Crafts metalworking business in Liverpool gradually disposed of it as he moved to London to take over the

metalwork department at the newly established Sir John Cass Technical Institute, becoming Head of its Art School as well as teaching at the London County Council Central School of Arts and Crafts. He exhibited metalwork and jewellery at the Arts and Crafts Exhibitions.

Robinson, Frederick Cayley (1862-1927)
Born in Brentford, Middlesex, he studied at the Royal Academy Schools from 1884, painted on a yacht for two years, then studied at the Académie Julian in Paris from 1890 to 1892. He exhibited at the Royal Society of British Artists from 1888, when he was elected Member and at the Royal Academy from 1895, to which he was elected Associate in 1921; he was also elected to the Royal Institute of Oil Painters in 1906; the New English Art Club in 1912; and the Royal Society of Painters in Water-colours in 1918, becoming its Vice-President from 1920 to 1923. His first one-man show was in 1908 at the Carfax Gallery in London. He was Professor of Figure Composition and Decoration at the Glasgow School of Art from 1914 to 1924, designed the decor and costumes for Maurice Maeterlinck's Symbolist play *The Blue Bird* at the Haymarket Theatre in London in 1909 and illustrated several books, including *The Blue Bird* and *The Book of Genesis* with mysterious, elliptical images.

ROYAL DOULTON   John Doulton (1793-1873) was apprenticed to a stoneware pottery in Fulham at the age of twelve. On completing his apprenticeship in 1812 he went to work for a small pottery in Vauxhall Walk, near Lambeth, owned by a widow, Martha Jones, and run by John Watts as manager. Three years later Mrs Jones offered partnerships to Watts and Doulton; she retired in 1820 and Watts in 1853, after which the company was renamed Doulton and Co., expanding its production of chemical and domestic stoneware, terracotta vessels and salt glazed stoneware sanitary fittings to include art wares at its new factories in Lambeth and Burslem, including painted porcelain. The Company was run by John's son, Henry Doulton (1820-1897), knighted in 1887, and the recipient of a vast collection of medals and honours from various international exhibitions. He was succeeded by his son Lewis Doulton in 1897, and he turned the firm into a limited company in 1899 which received a Royal Warrant from King Edward VII two years later, enabling the word 'Royal' to be added to the firm's name. Lewis Doulton resigned in 1919 and the new Managing Director was Sir Henry's grandson, Lewis Eric Hooper, who became Chairman from 1925 to 1955. Art Nouveau designs were created by several artists, particularly Mark V. Marshall (1879-1912), who began as a stone carver on Victorian Gothic Churches before joining the Lambeth Studio in 1879, skilfully carving the wet clay to produce dragons, snakes and lizards entwined around many of his pots; Eliza Simmance (1873-1928), a stylish and prolific designer who kept several assistants working full-time on her designs, and used a variety of techniques, including coloured slip decoration, carving, perforating and pâte-sur-pâte; Margaret Thompson (1889-1926)who decorated a number of wares in Art Nouveau style, but also specialised in painting individual ceramic tiles and complete ceramic tile murals with scenes from legends, nursery rhymes and children's stories for use in hospital wards, particularly children's wards; and Francis C. Pope (1880-1925), who modelled a number of stoneware vases in relief with mermaids, nymphs and other Art Nouveau images which were then given a metallic lustre finish using an electroplating technique to give both silver and copper finishes which he perfected, as well as developing leopard skin glazes. Charles J. Noke (1889-1936) left the Worcester Porcelain Company and joined Doulton in 1889 at the invitation of the Art Director, John Slater. The two men worked closely together, and Noke later became Art Director. He personally modelled many vases, but also introduced many new lines, from the sombre Rembrandt and Holbein wares to the delicate pale colours of Titanium ware, a glaze composed of titanium oxide which could be used on the finest porcelain, as well as Chinese Jade wares, Crystalline wares and figurines. His most spectacular achievement was the development of high temperature transmutation glazes in the style of the great Chinese potters. He brought in Bernard Moore (1850-1935), who had built up his family firm's production of fine china till it rivalled Minton, then sold it at the turn of the century to begin a new career

as glaze chemist and technical consultant to the china trade as well as setting up a small decorating studio in Stoke-on-Trent. Noke, Moore and Cuthbert Bailey carried out innumerable experiments using a copper based glaze and a reducing kiln, eventually developing a rich red glaze which was called Rouge Flambé, a range that was introduced to great acclaim at the St. Louis International Exhibition in the United States in 1904. Further experiments with transmutation glazes produced the Sung wares, developed during the First World War, which extended the range of colours and created mottled, feathered and veined effects on the Flambé bodies. But the most spectacular range of transmutation glaze ceramics were the Chang Wares in which a fairly massive body was covered in a gloppy glaze in brilliant colours which was allowed to dribble down the body, its rich, velvety lustre creating a unique vessel which could not be duplicated. Although the line was only commercially introduced in 1925 and abandoned in 1939, most of its production is truly Art Nouveau in its conception, inspiration and realisation.

Smith, Gertrude   Jeweller and enameller. She had a Studio in London at 52 Rathbone Place, W.1, across Oxford Street from Soho.

SOPER, WILLIAM   William Soper & Son was a commercial firm of 'jewellers and art enamellers' established in Poland Street in Soho with retail premises at 136 Ebury Street, S.W. The firm executed enamels and jewellery to order, remounted and reset stones and executed repairs, and displayed their sign "By Appointment to H.R.H. Princess Christian."

Southall, Joseph Edward (1861-1944) Born in Nottingham, he trained for four years in a Birmingham architectural office. On a visit to Italy in 1883 he discovered tempera painting, and was largely responsible for its revival. Encouraged by Burne-Jones, he taught at the Birmingham School of Art and executed frescos in the Birmingham City Art Gallery and the Council House. He was elected to the Royal Society of Painters in Water-colours in 1931, and was President of the Royal Birmingham Society of Artists.

Stabler, Harold (1872-1945) Having studied woodwork and stone carving at the Kendal School of Art, he taught at the Keswick School of Industrial Arts. In 1899 he went to the Liverpool University Art School where he joined the metalworking department headed by R. Llewellyn Rathbone. He met his future wife Phoebe McLeish (d. 1955) there: she had trained as a sculptor at Liverpool University and the Royal College of Art in London. Harold Stabler moved to the Sir John Cass Technical Institute in London with Rathbone in 1906 and succeeded him as Head of its Art School between 1907 and 1937. He worked as a silversmith and enameller, designed for steel and glass, and was a founder member of the Design and Industries Association in 1915. Together the Stablers designed ceramic figures and plaques, some of which were produced in small editions by the pottery firm of Carter, Stabler and Adams, of which he was a co-founder. Phoebe Stabler exhibited sculpture in bronze, stone and terracotta at the Royal Academy, the Royal Society of Portrait Painters, the Royal Glasgow Institute of Fine Arts, the Women's International Art Club, in the provinces and abroad, and was elected Member of the Royal Society of British Sculptors in 1923.

Steele, Florence (Fl.1895-1918)   Studied design and modelling under Lanteri at the South Kensington Schools from 1892 to 1896, winning a Gold Medal in 1894 and a National Scholarship. She executed a variety of small-scale objects, including jewellery, mirrors, caskets and book-bindings in silver, bronze or plaster, often decorated in low relief, which she exhibited with the Arts and Crafts Exhibition Society. She was commissioned by the Art Union of London and employed as designer by Elkington and Pilkington.

Toft, Albert (1862-1949)   Born in Birmingham, he was apprenticed as modeller at Elkington & Co then at Wedgwood. He went to art schools at Henley and Newcastle-under-Lyme before entering the South Kensington Schools as a National Scholar to study modelling with Lanteri. He executed many monuments and portrait and decorative sculptures as well as some small-scale

right:
Albert Toft, Imploration,
bronze

far right:
*Dante Gabriel Rossetti,
A Stunner holding a Leaf,
Coloured crayon in Rossetti
frame*

Symbolist works. He joined the Art Workers' Guild in 1891.

Varley, Charles Fleetwood (1881-1969) Member of a family of painters, he executed painted enamel landscape and seascape plaques which were incorporated into the lids of silver and pewter boxes by Liberty & Co and the Guild of Handicraft. He also produced copper boxes set with enamel plaques and made some jewellery.

Watt, James Cromar (1862-1940) Scottish jeweller, working in Aberdeen, who specialised in making necklaces, boxes, lockets and pendants in gold, cloisonné-enamelled over foil. He often used the motif of entwined snakes, and set them with pearls, garnets, opals, moonstones, carved lapis lazuli or Mexican fire opals.

Wiens, Stephen M. (1871-1956) Born Siegfried Wiens in London to German parents, he studied art at the Royal Academy Schools from 1890 onwards, although he was partly educated in Germany. As a painter and sculptor of portraits and figure subjects he exhibited at the Royal Academy from 1893. He changed his first name to Stephen in 1920. A cast of his sculpture of *The Girl and the Lizard* is in the Tate Gallery, London, part of the Chantry Bequest.

Wilson, Henry (1864-1934) After studying architecture under John Oldrich Scott and John Belcher, he became chief assistant to J.D. Sedding, who had designed the Church of the Holy Redeemer in Clerkenwell, then the Holy Trinity Church in Sloane Street, although he died before the completion of the interior. Wilson completed the project, in which William Morris, Burne-Jones, Nelson Dawson and the sculptors Edward Onslow Ford, Alfred Gilbert, Henry Bates, Hamo Thornycroft and Frederick W. Pomeroy were involved. As he became more interested in metalwork, he set up a metal-working studio in about 1895, where he designed jewellery and some silver, which was executed by several very able assistants, including H.G. Murphy, Sydney Wiseman, Herbert Maryon, Latino Movio and Lorenzo Colarossi, the latter two of whom trained John Paul Cooper (1869-1933) who was apprenticed to Wilson. Wilson taught for a while at the Central School of Arts and Crafts, where he had a brief partnership with his fellow teacher Alexander Fisher, then taught at the Royal College of Art from 1901. Two years later he published *Silverwork and Jewellery*, a detailed manual. He joined the Art Workers' Guild in 1892, and became Master in 1937. He selected the jewellery that was exhibited at the Paris Exhibitions in 1914 and 1925. He designed the bronze doors for the Cathedral of St. John the Divine in New York in 1905. After the First World War he devoted himself largely to architectural sculpture.

Wood, Francis Derwent (1871-1926) Born in Keswick, he studied at Karlsruhe in Germany, returning to England in 1889. He worked as modeller for the ceramics firm of Maw & Co and the Coalbrookdale Iron Co, then attended the South Kensington Schools as a National Scholar studying under Lanteri, after which he became an assistant to Alphonse Legros at the Slade School, entered the Royal Academy Schools in 1894 as an assistant to Thomas Brock, winning a Gold Medal and travelling studentship the following year and went to Paris. He was appointed modelling master at the Glasgow School of Art and there won a competition for decorative sculpture at the Glasgow Art Gallery in 1899. He executed many memorials, architectural and portrait sculpture, and small scale Symbolist sculpture. He was Professor of Sculpture at the Royal College of Art between 1918 and 1923, joined the Art Workers' Guild in 1901, was elected Full Member of the Royal Academy in 1920 and was a founder member of the Royal Society of British Sculptors.

BIBLIOGRAPHY

Alison, Filippo: *Mackintosh as a Designer of Chairs*, London 1978

Anscombe, Isabelle: *Arts and Crafts Style*, New York 1991

Anscombe, Isabelle & Charlotte Gere: *Arts and Crafts in Britain and America*, London 1978

The Antique Trader: *The Liberty Style*, London 2000

The Art Journal

Arwas, Victor & Anthony Jones: *The Liberty Style*, Tokyo 1999

Arwas, Victor: *Liberty Style*, Tokyo 1983

Bilcliffe, Roger: *Charles Rennie Mackintosh: The Complete Furniture*, Guildford & London 1979, 1980, 1986

Bilcliffe, Roger: *Mackintosh Furniture*, Cambridge 1984

Bilcliffe, Roger: "J.H. McNair in Glasgow and Liverpool" in *Walker Art Gallery Annual Report and Bulletin*, Liverpool 1970-1

Birmingham City Museum and Art Gallery: *Birmingham Gold and Silver 1783-1973*, Birmingham 1973

Brett, David: *C.R. Mackintosh – The Poetics of Workmanship*, London 1992

Brighton Museum: *Beauty's Awakening, The Centenary Exhibition of the Art Workers' Guild 1884-1984*, Brighton 1984

Burkhauser, Jude (ed.): *Glasgow Girls – Women in Art and Design 1880-1920*, Edinburgh 1990

Callen, Anthea: *Angel in the Studio*, London 1979

Calloway, Stephen: *Liberty of London*, London 1992

Catalogue of an Exhibition of Doulton Pottery, London, Part 1 1971; Part 2 1975

Charles Rennie Mackintosh Society *Newsletter*

Connoisseur

Cooper, Jackie (ed.) *Mackintosh Architecture*, London 1978

Crawford, Alan (ed.): *By Hammer and Hand: The Arts and Crafts Movement in Birmingham*, Birmingham nd

Crawford, Alan: *Charles Rennie Mackintosh*, London 1995

Cumming, Elizabeth: *Glasgow 1900*, Amsterdam 1993

Davidson, Fiona: *Charles Rennie Mackintosh*, Andover 1998

Dekorative Kunst

Deutsche Kunst und Dekoration

Dorment, Richard: *Alfred Gilbert*, New Haven & London 1985

Elzea, Rowland & Betty: *The Pre-Raphaelite Era 1848-1914*, Wilmington, Delaware, 1976

The Fine Art Society: *Sculpture in Britain 1850-1914* (Introduction by Lavinia Handley-Read), London 1968

The Fine Art Society: *The 1933 Memorial Exhibition – A Reconstruction*, Glasgow 1983

The Fine Art Society: *Gibson to Gilbert*, London 1992

The Fine Art Society: *Mackintosh & The Vorticists*, London 1993

Gere, Charlotte: *Victorian Jewellery Design*, London 1972

Gere, Charlotte & Geoffrey C. Munn: *Artist's Jewellery – Pre-Raphaelite to Arts and Crafts*, Suffolk 1989

Gere, Charlotte & Michael Whiteway: *Nineteenth Century Design from Pugin to Mackintosh*, London 1993

Glasgow Museums and Art Galleries: *Glasgow School of Art Embroidery 1894-1920*, Glasgow 1980

Glasgow Museums and Art Galleries: *The Glasgow Style 1890-1920*, Glasgow 1984

Glasgow School of Art: *Charles Rennie Mackintosh*, 1961

Glasgow School of Art: *Charles Rennie Mackintosh Furniture*, nd

Glasgow School of Art: *Charles Rennie Mackintosh Ironwork & Metalwork*, nd

Helland, Janice: *The Studios of Frances and Margaret Macdonald*, Manchester & New York 1996

Howarth, Thomas: *Charles Rennie Mackintosh and the Modern Movement*, London 1952, 1977, 1990

Hunterian Art Gallery: *Margaret Macdonald Mackintosh*, Glasgow 1984

Irvine, Louise & Paul Atterbury: *Gilbert Bayes, Sculptor 1872-1953*, London 1998

Jones, Anthony: *Charles Rennie Mackintosh*, London 1990

Kaplan, Wendy (ed.): *Charles Rennie Mackintosh*, Glasgow & New York 1996

Larner, Gerald & Celia: *The Glasgow Style*, Edinburgh 1979

McAllister, Isabel: *Alfred Gilbert*, London 1929

Macleod, Robert: *Charles Rennie Mackintosh*, London 1968, 1983

The Magazine of Art

Manning, Elfrida: *Marble and Bronze, The Art and Life of Hamo Thornycroft*, London, 1982

Martin, Stephen A. (ed.): *Archibald Knox*, London 1995

Maryon, Herbert: *Modern Sculpture*, London 1933

Pevsner, Nikolaus & J.M. Richards (ed.): *The Anti-Rationalists*, London 1976

Read, Benedict & Joanna Barnes (ed.): *Pre-Raphaelite Sculpture*, London, 1991

Robertson, Pamela (ed.): *Charles Rennie Mackintosh: The Architectural Papers*, Wendlebury, 1990

Robertson, Pamela: *The Estate and Collection of Works by Charles Rennie Mackintosh at the Hunterian Art Gallery, University of Glasgow*, Glasgow 1991

Scottish Arts Council: *Charles Rennie Mackintosh – A Centenary Exhibition* (Introduction by Andrew McLaren Young), 1968

Spielmann, M.H.: *British Sculpture and Sculptors of Today*, London 1901

The Studio

Tilbrook, A.J. & Gordon House: *The Designs of Archibald Knox for Liberty & Co.*, London 1976

Turner, Mark et al: *Art Nouveau Designs from the Silver Studio Collection*, London 1986

Turner, Mark et al: The Silver Studio Collection, London 1980

Victoria & Albert Museum: *Liberty's 1875-1975*, London 1975

CREDITS

Back cover   Wigmore Hall, London,
Photographer Peter Aprahamiam
1   Arwas archives
2   John Jesse, London
3   Victor and Gretha Arwas, London
6-7   Photo, The Glasgow Picture Library
8   Phillips, London
10-11 © Hunterian Art Gallery, University of
Glasgow, MackintoshCollection. Photo, Media
Services Photographic, University of Glasgow
12   Tadema Gallery, London
13   Victor and Gretha Arwas, London
14   Photo, Glasgow School of Art
15   The Fine Art Society, London
16   Arwas archives
17   Above left: Private Collection, London
Above right: Victor and Gretha Arwas, London
18   Sotheby's London
20-21 The Fine Art Society, London
22   Victor and Gretha Arwas, London
23   Victor and Gretha Arwas, London
24   Above left: Victor and Gretha
Arwas, London
Above right: The Fine Art Society London
25   The Fine Art Society, London
26   Above: Private collection, London
Above right: Private collection
Right: Victor and Gretha Arwas, London
27   Victor and Gretha Arwas, London
28   Sotheby's, London
29   The Fine Art Society, London
30   The Fine Art Society, London
31   The Fine Art Society, London
32   Sotheby's, London
33   The Fine Art Society, London
34   Sotheby's, London
35   The Fine Art Society, London
36   Right: The Glasgow Picture Library.
Photo, Eric Thorburn
Below right: © Hunterian Art Gallery,
University of Glasgow, Mackintosh
Collection. Photo, Michael Kuznack
37   © Hunterian Art Gallery, University of
Glasgow, Mackintosh Collection
38   The Fine Art Society, Edinburgh
39   The Fine Art Society Archive
40   Above: The Glasgow Picture Library.
Photo, Eric Thorburn
Above right: The Glasgow Picture Library.
Photo, Eric Thorburn
Right: © Hunterian Art Gallery,
University of Glasgow, Mackintosh Collection
41   The Fine Art Society, London
42   The Fine Art Society, London
43   Sotheby's, London
44   Above: Victor and Gretha Arwas, London
Above right: Private collection, London
Right: Victor and Gretha Arwas, London
45   Sotheby's London
46   Christie's, London
47   Paul Lincoln
48   © Hunterian Art Gallery, University of
Glasgow, Mackintosh Collection
49   The Fine Art Society, London
50   Above right: The Fine Art Society, London

51   The Fine Art Society, London
52   Sotheby's, London
53   Private collection, London
54   Above: Victor and Gretha Arwas, London
Right: Private collection, London
55   © Hunterian Art Gallery, University of
Glasgow, Mackintosh Collection
56   The Fine Art Society, London
57   The Fine Art Society, London
58   Above: The Fine Art Society, London
Right: Glasgow Picture Gallery.
Eric Thorburn photographer
59   The Fine Art Society, London, London
60   © Hunterian Art Gallery, University of
Glasgow, Mackintosh Collection
61   Glasgow Picture Gallery. Eric Thorburn
62   Above: © Hunterian Art Gallery,
University of Glasgow, Mackintosh Collection
Right: The Fine Art Society, London
63   The Fine Art Society, London
64   Left: The Fine Art Society, London
Right: The Fine Art Society, London
65   The Fine Art Society, London
67   © Hunterian Art Gallery, University of
Glasgow, Mackintosh Collection
68   © Hunterian Art Gallery, University of
Glasgow, Mackintosh Collection
69   © Hunterian Art Gallery, University of
Glasgow, Mackintosh Collection
70   Private collection
72   John Jesse, London
73   Sotheby's, London
74   Victor and Gretha Arwas, London
75   Arwas archive
76   Above left: Victor and Gretha Arwas
Above right: Phillips, London
Right: Victor and Gretha Arwas
77   Above left: Phillips, London
Above right: Private collection
Right: Private collection
79   Above left: Victor and Gretha Arwas, London
Above right: The Fine Art Society, London
Below: Arwas archives
80   Above left: The Liberty Collection
Above right: Victor and Gretha Arwas, London
Below: Private collection
81   Private collection
82   Above: Private collection
Right: Tadema Gallery, London
84   Left and right: Private collection
85   Left and right: Private collection
87   Phillips, London
88   Right: Phillips, London
89   Above: Phillips, London
Below left and right: Victor and Gretha
Arwas, London
90   Above left and right: Victor and Gretha
Arwas, London
91   Above left and right: Victor and Gretha
Arwas, London
92   Victor and Gretha Arwas, London
93   Victor and Gretha Arwas, London
94   Victor and Gretha Arwas, London
95   Victor and Gretha Arwas, London
96   Victor and Gretha Arwas, London

97   Above: Private collection
Below: John Jesse, London
98   Above and right: John Jesse, London
99   John Jesse, London
100   Victor and Gretha Arwas, London
101   Victor and Gretha Arwas, London
102   Victor and Gretha Arwas, London
103   Victor and Gretha Arwas, London
104   Victor and Gretha Arwas, London
105   Private collection
106   Victor and Gretha Arwas, London,
except top row, 3rd from left, Barbara
Macklowe, New York
107   Victor and Gretha Arwas, London
108   Arwas archives
109   Above and right: Privat collection
110   Victor and Gretha Arwas, London
111   Arwas archives
112   Above left: Victor and Gretha Arwas
Above right: Private collection
Right: Private collection
113   Private collection
114   Above left: Victor and Gretha Arwas
Right, centre and below: Arwas archives
115   Above and right: Arwas archives
116   Above: Arwas archives
Right: Victor and Gretha Arwas, London
117   Above: John Jesse, London
Right: Victor and Gretha Arwas, London
118-9 Private collection, London
120   Above: John Jesse, London
Right: Nicholas Harris, London
121   Above: John Jesse, London
Below left and centre: Onn Tammuz, London
Below right: Private collection
122   Arwas archives
123   Above: Private collection, London
Below: Nicholas Harris, London
124   Above: Arwas archives
Right: Nicholas Harris, London
125   Arwas archives
126   The Liberty Collection, London
127   Private collection
128   Left and right: Private collection
129   Private collection
130   Above and below: Arwas archives
131   Above left, centre and right: John Jesse, London
Right: Private collection, London
133   Victor and Gretha Arwas, London
135   Above: The Purple Shop
Below: Victor and Gretha Arwas, London
136   The Liberty Collection
137   The Liberty Collection
138   The Antique Trader at the Millinery Works
139   Private collection
140   The Liberty Collection
141   Fay Lucas Gallery
142   Above: The Liberty Collection
Right: Galerie Maria de Beyrie, Paris
143   The Antique Trader at the Millinery Works
145   Victor and Gretha Arwas, London
146   Above: Hida Takayama Museum of Art,
Japan
Right: The Fine Art Society
147   Above left and right: Tadema Gallery, London

148   Tadema Gallery, London
149   Tadema Gallery, London
150   Above and right: Tadema Gallery, London
151   Above and right: Tadema Gallery, London
152   Arwas archives
154   Victor and Gretha Arwas, London
155   Above left, centre and right: Victor and
Gretha Arwas, London
156   Right and below: Victor and Gretha Arwas,
London
157   Arwas archive
158   Above left and right: Victor and Gretha
Arwas, London
Right: Private collection
159   Above left: Private collection, London
Above right: Nicholas Harris, London
Right: Victor and Gretha Arwas, London
160   Above left and right: Nicholas Harris, London
Right: Victor and Gretha Arwas, London
161   Above left and right: Nicholas Harris, London
Right: Victor and Gretha Arwas, London
162   Victor and Gretha Arwas, London
163   Background and above: Nicholas Harris,
London
164   Above and right: Nicholas Harris, London
165   The Birkenhead Collection
166   Above and below: Victor and Gretha
Arwas, London
167   The Fine Art Society, London
168   Above left: Nicholas Harris, London
Above right: Phillips, London
Right: Nicholas Harris, London
169   Above: The Fine Art Society, London
Right: Nicholas Harris, London
170   The Fine Art Society, London
171   Victor and Gretha Arwas, London
172   Victor and Gretha Arwas, London
173   Above: Nicholas Harris, London
Right: Victor and Gretha Arwas, London
174   Period photograph
175   Victor and Gretha Arwas, London
176   Nicholas Harris, London
177   Nicholas Harris, London
178   Above and right: Sotheby's, London
179   Above left, centre and right: Victor and
Gretha Arwas, London
Below: The Fine Art Society, London
180   The Fine Art Society, London
181   Victor and Gretha Arwas, London
182   Above: The Fine Art Society, London
Right: Whitford and Hughes, London
183   Above: Victor and Gretha Arwas
Right: Private collection
184   Above: Royal Academy of Arts, London
Below: Victor and Gretha Arwas, London
185   Arwas archives
187   Right: The Fine Art Society, London
Far right: Victor and Gretha Arwas, London
189   Right: The Fine Art Society, London
Far right: Victor and Gretha Arwas, London
191   Right and far right: Private collection
193   Forbes Magazine Collection, The Fine Art
Society, London
197   Right: Victor and Gretha Arwas, London
Far right: Arwas archives

INDEX

Artificers' Guild 170, 187, 188, *148, 150*

Ashbee, C.R. 114,185,191,*147*

Baker, Oliver 186, *96, 129*

Bates, Harry 186

Bayes, Gilbert 186, 187

Beardsley, Aubrey 24

Beggarstaff, J. & W. *152*

Blackie,Walter W. 56

Blizard, F.S 13

Benson, W.A.S. 186, 160

Brannam, C.H. 101, 104

Brock, Thomas 186, *187*

Brown, Ford Madox 78, 187

Browning, Robert Barrett 186, *183*

Burges, William 86

Burne-Jones, Edward 75,78,187,189

Burns, Robert 71, 187, *70*

Century Guild 83, 114

Clutha Glass 67, 104, 140, *124*

Coleman, W.S. 101

Cooper, John Paul 187, *147*

Couper & Sons, James 67, 104

Crane, Walter 12, 101, 187

Cranston, Miss Catherine 34, 67,

Davidson, George Dutch 71

Dawson, Nelson & Edith 170-171, 188, 189, *75, 112*

Dean, A. *76*

De Morgan, William 83, 101, *77, 80*

Doulton, Royal 144, 195, *76, 77, 87, 89, 113*

Dresser, Christopher 67, 91, 101, 104

Drury, Alfred 189

Duncan, John 71

Eadie, Kate 170, 189, 194, *172*

Ednie, John 60

Fisher, Alexander 166, 167, 170, 188, 189, *146, 168, 169, 170, 178*

Fitchew, Dorothy 189, *84, 85, 155*

Foley Potteries *158*

Ford, Edward Onslow 12, 189, *189*

Frampton, George 13, 186, 190, *147, 184*

Garbe, Louis Richard *179*

Gaskin, Arthur & Georgina 153, 190, *112, 149*

Gilbert, Sir Alfred 12, 190, *79, 180, 182, 183, 189*

Gilmour, Margaret 190, *47, 50, 52*

Gleaner, Percy *159*

Guild of Handicraft 185, *79, 147, 163*

Haité, G.C. 190, *79*

Harris, Kate 191

Hartwell, Charles Leonard *179*

Heaton, Clément 83

Henry, J.S. 186, *81*

Herkomer, Sir Hubert 170, *166*

Holiday, Henry 170, 191, *172*

Hunt, William Holman 74

Image, Selwyn 83

Ingram, Walter Rowlands *181*

Jack, George Washington 78

Jackson, F. Hamilton 191, *156*

Jones, A.E. 190, 191, *164*

Keppie, Jessie 24, 49

Keswick School of Industrial Art *82*

King, Jessie M. 34, 56-67, 192, *22, 23, 24, 25, 26, 27, 53, 89, 150, 184*

Knight, Dame Laura *171*

Knox, Archibald 122, 185, 192, *3, 90, 91, 92, 93, 94, 95, 97, 98, 99, 100, 101, 102, 103, 105, 106, 108, 109, 110, 111, 114, 115, 116, 117, 118-119, 120, 121, 122, 123, 124, 125, 126, 127, 128, 130, 131, 135, 143*

Leighton, Frederick, Lord *179*

Logan, George 60

Mackintosh, Charles Rennie 16, 20-67, *1, 6-7, 14, 15, 18, 29, 30, 31, 32, 33, 34, 35, 36, 37, 38-39, 40, 41, 42, 43, 45, 50, 51, 58, 59, 60, 61, 64, 65, 66*

Mackintosh, Margaret Macdonald 16, 21, 24, 28, 42, 53, *48, 49, 58, 64, 68*

Mackennal, Sir Bertram 192, *179, 182*

McNair, Frances Macdonald 16, 20, 21, 24, 28, 53, 56, *8, 10-11, 54, 55, 57, 62, 63, 64, 69, 191*

McNair, Herbert 16, 20, 21, 24, 28, 53, 56, *64, 191*

March Brothers 192-193, *17*

Marks, Gilbert 193, *161, 163*

Marriott, Pickford 193, *72, 73*

Meteyard, Sidney 153, 167, 170, 189, 194, *173*

Minton 101, *88*

Moira, Gerald 194, *Back Flap*

Moorcroft 144, *76*

Moore, Bernard 196, *160*

Morris, Talwin 46, 56

Morris, William 28, 75, 78, 86, 87, 104, 185, 186, 187, *72-73, 146*

Muthesius, Hermann 42

Naper, Ella 194, *82*

Neatby, W.J. 194, *155*

Newberry, Francis 19, 20, 21, 28, 34, 43, 52, 56

Partridge, Fred 195, *12, 112, 151*

Powell & Sons, Whitefriars 105, 140, 187, *109, 125, 128, 185*

Pugin, A.W.N. 75

Rackham, Arthur *157*

Ramsden & Carr 195, *112*

Richmond, Sir William Blake 12

Rossetti, Dante Gabriel 42, 75, 78, 91, 187, *197*

Rowat, Jessie 20

Ruskin, John 86, 144

Ruskin Pottery 153, *158*

Sedding, John Dando 75

Shaw, Myra *158*

Shaw, Norman 75

Simpson, Edgar *157*

Smith, John Moyr 86, 101, *160, 161*

Solon, Léon Victor *88*

Southall, Joseph 153, 196

Spencer, Edward 170, 188, *150*

Stabler, Harold & Phoebe 196

Steele, Florence 196, *162*

Stoddart, John McKay *46*

Talbert, Bruce 86

Taylor, E.A. 60-67, 100, 192, *26, 89, 138, 139*

Thew, Mary *44*

Thompson, Margaret E. 196, *89*

Toft, Albert 196, *197*

Traquair, Phoebe Anna 171, 189, *173, 176, 177*

Urushibara *155*

Voysey, C.F.A. 13, 86, 100, *165*

Walton, George 67, 100, 104

Watt, James Cromar 197, *44, 112*

Waugh, J.J. *154*

Webb, Philip 75, 78

Wien, S.M. 197, *17*

Wilmer, John Riley *156*

Womrath, Andrew 71

Wyburd, Leonard F. 100, *80, 140, 141, 142*